Don't Let the State Decide

Living Trusts, Wills & Estate Planning

for Aging Parents:

A Family Organizer's Roadmap to Protecting Assets and Avoiding Probate

M. Samuel Carrington

Disclaimer

The information contained in this book is for general informational purposes only. While every effort has been made to ensure the accuracy and reliability of the information provided, the author and publisher make no representations or warranties regarding the completeness, accuracy, reliability, or suitability of the information for any particular purpose.

The author and publisher do not assume responsibility for any errors, omissions, or any outcomes arising from the use of this information. Readers should consult with a qualified attorney or financial advisor before making any decisions related to trust, estate planning, wills, or legal matters.

This book is not intended as a substitute for legal, tax, or financial advice, and the author is not engaged in rendering legal, financial, or other professional advice or services.

Trademark Disclaimer

The trademarks, service marks, and logos used in this book, including the term “Living Trusts,” “Wills & Estate Planning,” and others mentioned, are the property of their respective owners. The use of any trademark or service mark in this book is solely for the purpose of providing examples and is not intended to suggest an affiliation, endorsement, or approval by the trademark owner.

All trademarks, logos, and product names are the property of their respective owners. The author and publisher disclaim any ownership or rights to any third-party trademarks used within the book.

Dedication

To families everywhere, who work tirelessly to protect the future and safeguard the legacies they have built. May this book guide you in your journey to ensure the well-being of your loved ones for generations to come.

Table of Contents

INTRODUCTION

You're Not Overreacting, You're Right to Be Worried

Why the adult child who picks up this book is usually the one holding everything together and why acting now changes everything.

The Person Who Always Ends Up Holding the Bag

You already know who you are.

You're the one who noticed your dad's mail piling up. The one who found out almost by accident that your mom doesn't have a will. The one who quietly Googled "living trust vs will" at 11 o'clock on a Tuesday night because nobody else in the family seemed concerned enough to do it.

Maybe you've tried to bring it up. Maybe you got a "we'll deal with it later" and a quick change of subject. Maybe your siblings think you're being morbid or pushy. Maybe your parents got defensive and you dropped it because you didn't want to start a fight.

And now you're reading this book.

That right there tells me something about you. You are the one who sees the problem before it becomes a crisis. The one who's willing to have uncomfortable conversation nobody else wants to touch. Here's what I want you to hear: you are not overreacting. You are not morbid. You are not being greedy by thinking about inheritance. You are doing exactly what a loving, responsible adult child should do — and you're doing it before it's too late.

That distinction matters more than most people realize.

Later Is a Fantasy

I've talked to thousands of families. Callers who waited too long. Callers who assumed the paperwork was handled. Callers sitting in hospital waiting rooms trying to figure out who has the legal authority to make a medical decision because nobody ever bothered to sign a healthcare directive.

The single most expensive word in estate planning is "later."

Not because death is coming tomorrow. But because the window for planning, the period when your parent is healthy, mentally sharp, and legally capable of signing documents is shorter than families think. And it closes fast. A stroke doesn't send a warning. A dementia diagnosis doesn't give you a grace period to get your affairs in order. By the time a lot of families realize they needed a plan, the moment to make one cleanly and easily has already passed.

What happens then? They end up in court. They end up paying attorneys thousands of dollars to get a judge to appoint a legal guardian because there's no power of attorney in place. They end up watching assets get eaten alive by probate a slow, public, expensive legal process that could have been avoided entirely with a simple living trust.

I've watched families lose more money to bad planning than they ever would have lost to taxes. And I've watched siblings who loved each other end up not speaking because nobody sat down and did the work while there was still time.

This book is about making sure that doesn't happen to your family.

Why This Conversation Feels So Hard

Let's be straight about something. Estate planning conversations are hard not because the legal stuff is complicated — it's not, and this book is going to prove that to you — but because they touch something much deeper than documents.

They touch mortality. They touch control. They touch old family dynamics that never got fully resolved. Your parent may hear "we need to talk about your estate plan" and what registers in their head is "you think I'm dying" or "you're already thinking about my money."

And you, on your end, may feel guilty for even bringing it up. Like you're being greedy. Like you're rushing something you're not supposed to rush.

Here's the truth: doing this work is not about the money. It's about love. It's about making sure that when your parent can no longer speak for themselves, their wishes are honored. It's about making sure that a lifetime of work — a house, savings, retirement accounts, maybe a small business or a piece of land — goes to exactly who they intended it to go to, without a court getting involved, without the family falling apart, and without the state making decisions your parent never authorized. Dying without a plan doesn't protect you from having a plan. It just means the state writes the plan for you. And I promise you, the state's plan is not what your parent would have chosen.

> *"It is an act of love to do your estate planning."*

I mean that. It is not morbid. It is not premature.

It is one of the most responsible, loving things a family can do together.

What This Book Is and What It Isn't

This is not a legal textbook. It's not written for attorneys. It's written for you, the adult child trying to figure out what your parents need, how to get the conversation started, and how to put the right documents in place before a crisis makes all of it much harder.

Each chapter is built around real situations. The kind of conversations that happen in kitchens and hospital rooms and attorneys' offices. The kind of problems that come up when nobody planned, and the kind of outcomes that happen when they do.

Part One, deals with the emotional reality before you ever say a word because if you walk into this conversation without understanding why it's so charged, you're going to do it wrong.

Part Two explains what your parents' needs in plain language, without the legal jargon. The difference between a will and a living trust. The five documents every aging parent must have. What happens to a family when there's no plan and a crisis hit.

Part Three gets into the money: how to take inventory of what your parents own, how to protect the home from nursing home costs, what Medicaid covers versus what most families assume it covers.

Part Four covers the situations that are genuinely complicated: cognitive decline, blended families, financial fraud, special needs dependents.

Part Five walks you through the actual setup process, step by step, including how to find and vet a qualified attorney without getting overcharged.

And Part Six covers what happens after the plan is in place — how to maintain it, update it, and execute it when the time comes.

By the time you finish this book, you will not be confused. You'll know what documents your parent's needs, why they need them, what happens without them, and how to get everything done.

The Silent Crisis Happening in Millions of Families Right Now

There's a staggering number of Americans over 65 who do not have a basic will. No living trust. No power of attorney. Nothing in place to protect their assets, their medical decisions, or the people they love.

And their adult children know it. They've been meaning to deal with it. They've thought about bringing it up. They're pretty sure mom has "something" from years ago that's probably outdated.

That's the silent crisis. Not the loud emergency, the quiet, creeping one. The plan that never got made. The conversation that never happened. The documents that were never signed.

By the time it becomes loud — a fall, a diagnosis, a sudden death — the options are narrower, the costs are higher, and the family is already under stress.

You picked up this book before that happened. That's not a small thing.

A Note on Wealth — This Applies to Everyone

I want to address something directly, because I hear this excuse all the time: "We don't have enough to worry about estate planning."

Wrong.

If your parent owns a home even a modest one, they need a plan. If they have a bank account, a retirement account, a life insurance policy, or a car, they need a plan. If they have opinions about who should make their medical decisions if they can't speak for themselves, they need a plan.

Estate planning is not a rich person's game. The families who get hurt worst by lack of planning are often middle-class families with modest assets — a house worth $250,000 that ends up going through probate at a cost of $15,000 to $30,000 in legal fees, just because nobody set up a living trust. A house that should have taken three weeks to transfer instead takes 18 months.

The amount of wealth involved does not change whether you need a plan. It changes how complex the plan is. This book covers both.

How to Use This Book

You can read it straight through or use it as a reference guide. The table of contents is detailed enough that you can jump directly to the chapter most relevant to your situation right now.

If the most pressing issue is starting the conversation with your parents, start with Part One.

If you're past the conversation and trying to understand what documents they need, jump to Part Two. If there's already a health crisis happening, go directly to Chapter 11.

And if you're worried about a sibling situation that's already getting complicated, Chapter 3 and Chapter 13 are where you want to be.

At the back of the book, you'll find appendices that function as working tools: a master document locator, a family asset inventory worksheet, a list of questions to ask an elder law attorney, a state-by-state probate guide, a plain-English glossary, and sample template forms.

This book is meant to be used, not just read. Write in the margins. Fill out the worksheets. Bring it to the conversation.

The Greatest Gift Is a Plan

Here's what I know after years of watching families navigate this: the ones who plan don't just protect their money. They protect their relationships. They protect their parents' dignity. They make an already hard time — the illness, the death, the grief — as clean and as simple as it can possibly be.

And they give their parents something priceless: the certainty that their wishes will be honored. That the house they worked 30 years to own won't be swallowed by a court process. That the grandchildren they wanted to leave something for will get it. That the sibling they trusted will have the legal authority to act when it matters.

That's not just financial planning. That's love made concrete. So, let's get to work.

CHAPTER 1

PART ONE: BEFORE YOU SAY A WORD

The Emotional Reality No Other Book Addresses

CHAPTER 1

Why This Conversation Feels Impossible

Before a single document gets signed, before an attorney is called, before the word "trust" gets spoken out loud in your parent's kitchen there is this: the conversation that most families cannot seem to start. This chapter is about why that is, and what it costs when it stays that way.

The Conversation Most Families Never Have

Somewhere in America right now, a parent in their seventies is watching television. They have a will drafted in 1998 that names an executor who died three years ago. Their bank accounts are in their own name only. Their adult children have no idea where the life insurance policy is, who the agent was, or whether the policy is even still active. And no one has talked about any of it.

This is not a story about a negligent family. It is the median story. Most American adults over 65 either have no estate plan at all, have documents so outdated they no longer reflect their actual wishes, or have a plan that exists on paper but has never been explained to the people who will need to execute it. Their adult children, meanwhile, are circling a conversation they cannot quite figure out how to start.

Estate planning gets framed as a financial or legal problem. It is neither, primarily. The reason most families do not have an adequate plan is not that they lack access to attorneys or money to pay for documents. The reason most families do not have an adequate plan is that the conversation required to create one touches things nobody wants to touch — mortality, control, money, family dynamics, fear — and the emotional weight of those subjects reliably defeats the practical urgency of the planning itself.

Understanding why the conversation feels impossible is not just an interesting psychological observation. It is the prerequisite for having it. You cannot navigate terrain you have not mapped.

> *Most families are not avoiding estate planning because it is complicated. They are avoiding it because it requires talking about things they have spent years not talking about.*

What Aging Parents Are Actually Afraid Of

The most common misreading adult children make about parental resistance is this: they think the resistance is about death. It is not. At least, not primarily.

Most aging parents have a more functional relationship with the idea of death than their children assume. People who have lived seven or eight decades have buried parents, siblings, spouses, friends. They have thought about death. Many have made their peace with the concept in ways that their children have not.

What they have not made peace with is the loss of control.

Estate planning, from a parent's perspective, is not fundamentally a conversation about dying. It is a conversation about who has it, who gives it up, and when. A parent who signs a durable power of attorney has just handed a legally enforceable document to another person that says: when I cannot manage my own affairs, this person decides for me. A parent who creates a trust and names a successor trustee has documented the exact conditions under which they become irrelevant to the management of everything they have built. A parent who names a healthcare agent has acknowledged that someone else will make life-or-death decisions on their behalf.

None of that is easy. It is not evasion to find it difficult. It is a normal human response to confronting the end of a long period of autonomy.

The adult child who approaches estate planning as a logistical problem to be solved is approaching it from a completely different frame than the parent who experiences it as a confrontation with their own diminishment. Those two frames talking past each other is the source of most of the frustration families report around this topic.

What the resistance looks like

Parental resistance to estate planning conversations shows up in recognizable patterns. The table below translates the surface language into what is usually underneath it.

What the Parent Says	What They Actually Mean
"I'm not ready to think about that."	Thinking about it makes the loss of control feel real and imminent.
"We already have a will. We're fine."	I handled this once and I'd like to believe it's done. Please don't reopen it.
"Your father handles all of that." / "Your mother knows where everything is."	I've delegated responsibility to avoid confronting the subject myself.
"Why are you asking about this now?"	I'm afraid of what your urgency implies about my health or proximity to death.
"That's between me and your father."	This feels like a boundary intrusion. I'm not ready to let my adult children into this part of my life.
"We don't have enough for it to matter."	I'm using perceived modesty of assets to avoid a conversation I don't want to have.
"I'll get to it."	I have no intention of getting to it anytime soon, but I want this conversation to end.

The pattern running through most of these responses is not hostility or indifference. It is self-protection. The conversation feels threatening in ways that are difficult for aging parents to articulate, and deflection is the most available tool for managing that threat.

Recognizing deflection for what it is — a signal that the conversation has touched something real rather than a final answer — changes how you respond to it. You are not hitting a wall. You are touching a nerve. Those are different things, and they call for different approaches.

Why Adult Children Wait

The resistance does not only live on the parent's side of the table. Adult children carry their own reasons for avoiding this conversation, and those reasons are worth examining honestly because they are often the actual explanation for why years pass without the planning getting done.

The guilt of seeming greedy

The fear of appearing to be interested in inheritance is one of the most powerful conversation-stoppers for adult children. Asking your parent about their estate plan feels and can look from the outside like asking what you're going to get when they die. That optic is uncomfortable enough that many adult children simply refuse to raise the subject, even when they know the absence of planning is creating real risk.

This is worth naming clearly: caring about whether your parent has an adequate estate plan is not the same thing as caring about the inheritance. It is caring about whether your parents' wishes will be honored, whether their care will be funded, whether the family will be protected from a legal crisis. Those are loving motivations. The discomfort about how they might look is worth working through rather than letting it dictate whether the conversation happens at all.

Denial about what's already happening

Some adult children avoid the estate planning conversation because having it would require acknowledging something they are not ready to acknowledge that their parent is aging, that their health may be declining, that the relationship as it has always existed is changing. The estate planning conversation is a concrete marker of that change. Avoiding it is a way of not accepting the change.

This form of avoidance is understandable and genuinely human. It is also, in practical terms, one of the more costly forms of delay. The families who wait until a health crisis forces the conversation are the ones most likely to find that the window for good planning has closed.

Cognitive decline does not announce itself on a schedule that accommodates family timelines.

Not wanting to upset the parents

Adult children who have watched the estate planning conversation go badly before who have raised the subject and been shut down, or who watched a sibling raise it and trigger a week-long silence develop a reasonable reluctance to try again. The short-term cost of the conversation feels certain. The long-term cost of not having it feels abstract.

What this calculus misses are that the cost of not having the conversation does not stay abstract. It becomes very concrete on a specific day, usually in a hospital waiting room or an attorney's office, when a family discovers that no plan exists and the decisions that needed to be made months or years earlier now must be put under pressure, without the time, information, or legal authority to make them well.

Genuine uncertainty about how to start

Some adult children are not avoiding the conversation for emotional reasons. They simply do not know how to start it in a way that does not immediately go wrong. What do you say? How do you raise the subject without triggering defensiveness? How do you frame it as coming from love rather than as an interrogation about assets? Chapter 2 addresses exactly this, with specific words and framings that open aging parents up rather than shutting them down.

The Silent Crisis Already in Progress

While families wait for the right moment to have this conversation, a set of consequences accumulates quietly in the background. None of them are loud. None of them announce themselves as problems yet. They are conditions that are building toward a crisis, and most families do not recognize them as such until the crisis has already arrived.

Documents that no longer reflect reality

The most common form of the silent crisis is a plan that exists but has decayed. The will names an executor who has since died. The retirement account beneficiary designation still names a spouse who passed away six years ago. The trust was funded when it was created but three bank accounts opened since then sit outside it in the parent's individual name. The healthcare directive was signed in a different state and names a healthcare agent who has since moved abroad.

None of these problems are visible from the outside. The parent believes the planning is done. The adult children believe the planning is done. Everyone has a vague sense that the documents exist. No one has read them recently, compared them against current assets, or verified that the named individuals are still living, still capable, and still appropriate for their roles.

The window that is closing

Estate planning has a window. On one side is the present moment, when a parent has full legal capacity, clear intentions, and the ability to sign documents that will hold up to scrutiny. On the other side is the point at which cognitive decline, serious illness, or sudden incapacity has made it impossible or legally questionable to create new documents.

The window does not close all at once. It closes gradually, and then sometimes very fast. A parent in the early stages of cognitive decline may still have full legal capacity to execute trust today and may not in six months. A parent in apparently good health may be hospitalized unexpectedly. The window is not visible from the outside, which is what makes waiting feel safe when it is not.

The cost that lands on the family

When a parent dies or loses capacity without an adequate plan in place, the cost does not disappear. It transfers. It becomes the adult children's problem: a probate proceeding that takes a year and costs tens of thousands of dollars, a conservatorship battle that forces the family into court to obtain authority they could have had with a simple document, a dispute among siblings about what the parent would have wanted that fractures relationships that were intact before the crisis hit.

These outcomes are not hypothetical. They are the regular, predictable results of inadequate planning, and they happen to families who loved their parents and meant to get to it. Meaning to get to it is not the same as getting to it.

> *The median estate settlement: Probate takes an average of nine to twenty-four months*

> *to complete, depending on the state and the complexity of the estate. Attorney fees alone often run 3 to 7 percent of the gross estate value. On a $400,000 estate, that is $12,000 to $28,000 in fees before a single dollar reaches a beneficiary. A revocable living trust that costs $2,500 to create eliminates most of that entirely.*

How to Know When Waiting Is No Longer an Option

There is a version of this subject where the urgency is always abstract where there is always technically more time, where the next visit will be a better moment, where it feels premature to push. That version of the subject is comfortable and wrong.

Several specific conditions signal that the planning needs to happen now rather than eventually. If any of these describe your parents' situation, eventually is already too late to be a safe plan.

Age 75 or older with no current plan

A parent over 75 with no estate plan, or with documents that have not been reviewed in more than five years, is in a statistically significant risk zone for both cognitive decline and serious health events. The combination of age-related risk and undocumented wishes is not a situation that improves with more time.

Any diagnosis affecting cognition

A diagnosis of mild cognitive impairment, early-stage dementia, Parkinson's disease, or any other condition affecting memory, judgment, or executive function changes the urgency of estate planning from high to immediate. Legal capacity is assessed now of signing a parent who can still execute valid documents today may not be able to in ninety days. This is not a reason to panic. It is a reason to call an elder law attorney this week.

A recent significant health event

A hospitalization, a fall, a diagnosis of serious illness, a surgery, any health event that surfaces the fragility of the current situation is also a natural opening for the estate planning conversation. The event provides context that makes the subject less threatening to raise you are not bringing it up out of nowhere. You are responding to something that just happened. Families that use these moments to move forward with planning are making a rational choice.

A named person in the plan has died or become incapacitated

If a named executor, trustee, DPOA agent, or beneficiary has died or is no longer able to serve, the plan has a structural gap that will surface at the worst possible time if it is not addressed.

A significant life change in the family

A divorce, a remarriage, a new grandchild, a child who has developed serious financial problems or a disability, a major change in the value of the estate — any of these can make an existing plan inadequate even if it was well-crafted when created. The plan reflects the family at a specific moment. When the family changes significantly, the plan needs to catch up.

> ***The clearest signal:*** *If you are reading this book, the conversation needs to happen. People do not read books about estate planning for aging parents because their parents' affairs are in perfect order. They read them because something has surfaced, a health scare, a family conversation that didn't go well, a sense of accumulating risk that has finally become impossible to ignore. That instinct is correct. Act on it.*

This Is an Act of Love

The estate planning conversation is hard because it is real. It is real in the way that very few conversations in a family's life are real — honest about aging, about loss, about what happens to the people you love after you are gone. Most families spend a lifetime avoiding exactly that level of honesty. Being asked to have it, in the kitchen on a Sunday afternoon, is genuinely difficult.

It is worth doing because of exactly that. The families that get through the awkwardness, the deflection, the discomfort, the moments where someone says something that lands wrong and everyone goes quiet — those families give their aging parents something rare: the knowledge that their wishes will be honored, that the people they love will be protected, and that the chaos they feared leaving behind will not materialize.

That is not a bureaucratic achievement. It is an act of love in the most practical form it can take. Chapter 2 moves from why the conversation is hard to how to have it — the specific words, framings, and approaches that open aging parents up rather than shutting them down.

CHAPTER 2

How to Start the Conversation Without Triggering a Fight

Knowing you need to have the conversation and knowing how to have it are two completely different things. This chapter gives you the language, the approach, and the contingency plans for when it doesn't go smoothly.

The First Thing to Understand

There is no perfect script for this conversation. Anyone who tells you otherwise hasn't spent much time around real families.

What there is, though, is a difference between approaches that tend to work and approaches that almost always backfire. The gap between them isn't usually about facts or logic — it's about timing, framing, and emotional intelligence. You can have every document name memorized and every statistic ready and still blow up the conversation in the first two minutes by leading the wrong way.

So before we get into specific language, here's the foundational principle: this conversation is not a transaction. You are not negotiating. You are not convincing. You are inviting your parent into a process that protects them, honors them, and gives them more control — not less — over what happens to everything they've built.

The moment you frame it that way in your own head, the words that come out of your mouth tend to change on their own.

The Words That Shut Parents Down

Language matters more in this conversation than most people expect. Certain phrases trigger an almost automatic defensive response in aging parents, regardless of how they're delivered. Knowing what they are helps you avoid them.

"When you die" or "after you're gone." This seems obvious in hindsight, but it's remarkable how often these phrases appear in otherwise well-intentioned conversations. Centering the conversation on death puts your parent in a position where they either must engage with their own mortality or deflect. Most deflect. Reframe around wishes, protection, and intention instead.

"You need to get this taken care of." Urgency reads as pressure. Pressure reads as control. Your parents spent a lifetime making their own decisions, and being told what they need to do even by a child they love activates resistance before you've made a single actual point.

"I've been worried about you." These feels caring, and it is. But it can also land as a signal that you've already made a judgment about their capacity or situation. Many parents hear it as: you don't think I'm handling things well. Start from curiosity rather than concern.

"What happens to the house?" or "What are you planning to leave us?" Even when this question comes from the most practical and loving place, it sounds like you're asking about your inheritance. Don't open there. Get to the financial specifics much later, after the relational and protective framing is firmly established.

"The lawyer said" or "I read that you should." External authority figures rarely help in this conversation. Your parents don't want to feel like they're being managed by a committee. You're having a family conversation, not presenting a legal brief.

The Words That Open Parents Up

The language that works tends to share a few common traits: it centers your parent's wishes rather than your concerns, it emphasizes their control rather than their vulnerability, and it frames the conversation as something you're doing together rather than something you're proposing to do to them.

Here are the phrases that tend to work, and what to replace them with:

> **Instead of:** *"When you die, what happens to the house?"*
>
> **Try:** *"I want to make sure your wishes are honored exactly the way you want, no matter what. Can we talk about what that looks like?"*
>
> **Instead of:** *"You need to get a will done."*
>
> **Try:** *"I'd love to understand what you've already thought about, so we can figure out together if anything needs to be updated."*
>
> **Instead of:** *"I've been worried about you."*
>
> **Try:** *"I've been thinking about our family a lot lately, and I want to make sure we're doing right by you."*

Instead of: *"What are you planning to leave us?"*

Try: *"What matters most to you about what happens to what you've built?"*

Notice the pattern. Every effective alternative center your parent as the decision-maker with values and intentions that deserve to be protected. You're not telling them what to do. You're asking them to articulate what they already want and then positioning the planning process as the vehicle that makes sure those wants are carried out.

> *Most parents, once they realize that estate planning is about protecting their wishes rather than surrendering control, become far more willing to engage.*

The Third-Party Story: Introducing Urgency Without Pressure

One of the most effective tools in this conversation is one you probably already have access to: a real story about another family.

Not a horror story designed to frighten your parents into action. A genuine example of what happens when a family doesn't have a plan in place — ideally one close enough to home to be relatable, but not so close that it feels like a personal accusation.

It might be a neighbor whose estate went through a long and expensive probate after they passed. A cousin whose family fought over the contents of the house because there was no will. A friend whose parents had a stroke and whose family spent months and thousands of dollars in court trying to get legal authority to manage their finances.

These stories do something that abstract warnings cannot: they make the risk concrete and human without making it personal. Your parents don't have to defend themselves or their choices. They can respond to the story with empathy, and that empathy becomes the opening.

From there, the transition is natural: "I'd hate for us to end up in a situation like that. I'd love to make sure we've got everything set up so that never happens to our family.

That's not pressure. That's love with a practical edge to it. And most parents can hear that.

Choosing the Right Setting

Where you have this conversation matters almost as much as how you have it.

Formal settings — sitting down at the kitchen table specifically to talk about estate planning tend to create formal energy. Your parents are arriving already a little guarded because they know what's coming. The conversation feels like a meeting rather than a family discussion, and meetings invite resistance.

The conversations that tend to go best happen in low-stakes, comfortable settings where the topic can come up naturally rather than be announced. A long car ride. A walk. Cooking together. Sitting on the back porch after dinner. These environments lower defenses and allow the conversation to breathe.

Timing matters too. Don't bring this up when your parents are tired, stressed, unwell, or already dealing with something difficult. Don't bring it up right before they must be somewhere. Give it room. A conversation this important deserves a relaxed hour, not a rushed fifteen minutes before someone must leave.

And do it one-on-one first. The initial conversation should be between you and your parents or between both parents if they're both present and you have a good relationship with both. Bringing siblings into the first conversation adds audience pressure and can make your parents feel outnumbered or managed. Siblings belong in later conversations, once the groundwork is laid.

When One Parent Is Willing and the Other Refuses

This is one of the most common and frustrating dynamics in estate planning conversations, and it deserves a direct answer.

Often there's an asymmetry: one parent frequently, the one who has thought more about the family's finances, or the one who has been more directly confronted with mortality through illness or the loss of peers is willing and even eager to put a plan in place. The other parent refuses, shuts down, or simply will not engage.

The worst thing you can do is try to force consensus before moving forward. If one parent is willing to update their documents, start there. A signed power of attorney, an updated will, a healthcare directive from one parent is meaningfully better than nothing while you continue working on the other.

For the resistant parent, the approach shifts. Stop trying to convince them directly that approach has already failed. Instead, try to understand the specific fear underneath the resistance. Is it loss of control? Is it superstition about acknowledging mortality? Is it distrust of attorneys? Is it disagreement with the other parent about what the plan should look like?

Each of these has a different solution. Loss of control responds to language that emphasizes their ongoing authority over every decision. Superstition responds to time often a resistant parent comes around after watching a friend's family navigate a crisis without a plan. Distrust of attorneys responds to education about the process and what an estate planning attorney does. Disagreement about the plan's content is a different conversation entirely and may benefit from a neutral third party — a financial advisor or attorney facilitating.

What rarely works: pushing harder. Bringing in more family members to apply social pressure. Framing the resistant parent's position as irresponsible or unfair to the family. These approaches entrench resistance rather than dissolving it.

> *The resistant parent is not your adversary. They're a person with a fear you haven't fully named yet. Find the fear, and you'll find the path forward.*

When a Health Event Has Just Occurred

A health scare, a fall, a hospitalization, a diagnosis — these events change the dynamics of this conversation significantly.

On one hand, they create a natural opening that didn't exist before. The abstract risk is suddenly concrete. Your parents have just had a direct encounter with their own vulnerability, and that encounter tends to make them more receptive to conversations they previously avoided. Many families find that a health event is the first moment a resistant parent genuinely becomes willing to engage.

On the other hand, the window after a health event is also when a parent's legal capacity may be most at risk. Pain medication, anesthesia, the cognitive effects of a hospitalization, the emotional weight of a serious diagnosis, all of these can affect whether your parent is in a condition to execute legal documents. A will or trust signed during a period of diminished capacity can be challenged later.

So, the approach after a health event is move with urgency, but also with care. Have the conversation while your parents are receptive. But before any documents are signed, consult with an elder law attorney about capacity, and consider a brief cognitive assessment if there's any question. The goal is documents that are legally bulletproof, not just signed.

Chapter 11 goes much deeper on cognitive decline and legal capacity. If you're reading this because a health event has already happened, go there next.

Conversation About What They Actually Want

Here's something that often gets skipped in the rush to get documents signed: the conversation about your parents' actual wishes.

Not the legal mechanics. The real stuff. What matters to them. Who they trust. What they've built that they're most proud of. What they'd hate to see happen after they're gone.

This conversation — which has nothing to do with attorneys or documents — is often the most important one you can have. It gives you a clear picture of what the plan is supposed to accomplish. It helps your parent feel heard and respected rather than processed. And it often surfaces wishes, concerns, and family dynamics that would never come out in a conversation framed around paperwork.

Some questions worth asking, in a low-pressure setting:

"If something happened and you couldn't make decisions for yourself, who would you want making them?"

"Is there anything specific you'd want to make sure stayed in the family?" "Is there anyone you'd want to make sure is taken care of?"

"Is there anything you'd definitely not want to happen?"

These questions are not leading. They don't presuppose a particular type of plan. They simply invite your parents to express what they want and that expression becomes the foundation everything else is built on.

An estate plan without this conversation is just paperwork. With it, it's a genuine reflection of your parents' life and values.

Ending the Conversation with Momentum

The single most common reason estate planning conversations fail to produce results is not that the conversation itself went badly. It's that it ended without a next step.

Your parents agreed that yes, this is important. You felt like real progress was made. And then a month went by and nothing happened because nobody identified a specific action to take before the conversation ended.

Every estate planning conversation should end with something concrete, even if it's small. Here's what that can look like at different stages:

If it's the first conversation and your parents are just beginning to warm up: agree to find out whether their current documents, if they exist, are up to date. Ask them to find the paperwork and agree to look at it together next time you talk.

If they're open to next steps but not sure where to start, offer to find two or three elder law attorneys in their area and get them names. Not to make the appointment for them but to give them options. Preserving their sense of agency at every step matters.

If they're ready to move, they agree on a date to schedule the attorney consultation before you leave. Not "soon." A date.

The momentum of this process is fragile in the early stages. Life gets busy. Discomfort returns. Without a specific next step tied to a specific timeline, even the best conversation fades back into "we'll deal with it later."

> ***Action principle:*** *Every conversation ends with one concrete next step and a timeline. Not a vague intention — a specific action and a specific date.*

When the Conversation Goes Badly

It will happen sometimes. Even with the right framing, the right setting, and the right language, some conversations hit a wall.

Your parents shut down. Get angry. Accuse you of being after their money. Leaves the room. Refuses to talk about it at all.

When this happens, the instinct is to push through or escalate. Resist that instinct. Pushing harder into a closed door doesn't open it. It just makes the door harder to open later.

Step back. Give it time — not months, but a few weeks. Let the emotional temperature come down. Then try again from a different angle, with different framing, at a different moment.

If the conversation has failed multiple times and the resistance is genuinely entrenched, consider involving a neutral third party. An elder law attorney who can frame the conversation in terms of protecting your parents' wishes rather than satisfying their children's concerns. A financial advisor your parents already trust. A pastor, a family friend, someone with credibility in your parent's eyes.

Sometimes the message lands differently from a different messenger. That's not a failure. That's just how people work.

And if none of it works? Document your efforts. Keep records of conversations and attempts. In the worst-case scenario, where your parents lose capacity without a plan in place, a record of good-faith attempts to address the situation can matter in court.

CHAPTER 3

The Sibling Problem: Getting Everyone on the Same Page

Estate planning doesn't just surface family tension — it amplifies whatever was already there. This chapter is about managing the sibling dynamic before it manages you.

Why Siblings Fight Before Anyone Has Even Died

It starts before the first document is signed. Sometimes before the first conversation with your parent has even happened.

A sibling finds out you've been talking to mom about her estate plan and immediately wants to know what was said, what was decided, and why they weren't included.

Another sibling who's been largely absent suddenly has very strong opinions about how things should be handled. The one who's provided most of the caregiving quietly seethes while the one who visits twice a year talks confidently about fairness and equal shares.

None of this is really about the estate plan. The estate plan is just the occasion. What's surfacing is decades of family history — perceived favoritism, old grievances, unresolved questions about who sacrificed what and who got away with what. Money and mortality have a way of making all of that louder.

Understanding this doesn't make the sibling dynamics easier to manage, but it does change how you respond to them. When a sibling reacts with suspicion or hostility to the estate planning process, you're not dealing with a rational objection that needs a rational answer. You're dealing with an emotional response rooted in something much older than this conversation. Responding to it at face value — as if it's about the documents — usually makes things worse.

> *The estate plan didn't create the family conflict. It just gave it somewhere to land.*

The Four Sibling Types You'll Encounter

Every family has its own specific cast of characters, but the sibling dynamics that come up in estate planning tend to follow a recognizable set of patterns. Knowing which type you're dealing with helps you choose the right approach.

The Uninvolved Sibling

This is the one who has been geographically or emotionally distant. They've contributed little to the day-to-day reality of your parent's life — few visits, minimal phone calls, no caregiving. But the moment estate planning enters the picture, they resurface with opinions. They want equal say in decisions they haven't been present for, and they may interpret any plan that doesn't treat them identically to more involved siblings as evidence of unfairness or manipulation. The approach here is transparency. Bring them into the process early, keep them informed, and document everything. Their disengagement does not disqualify them from the conversation, and trying to exclude them tends to backfire badly.

The Controlling Sibling

This one wants to run everything. They may have a financial or legal background that makes them confident they know best. They may simply have a personality that defaults to taking charge. The problem is that in estate planning, the only person whose wishes matter is your parent — and a controlling sibling who starts substituting their judgment for your parent's is a problem, not an asset. The solution is to keep your parent visibly and firmly at the center of every decision.

The attorney works for your parent, not for the family. Decisions get made based on what your parent wants, full stop. A controlling sibling who tries to redirect that tends to lose credibility quickly when it's framed that way clearly and consistently.

The Suspicious Sibling

This sibling assumes bad intent on someone's part — usually yours, if you're the one who initiated the planning conversation. They may believe you're trying to influence your parent's decisions in your favor, position yourself as the executor or trustee for personal gain, or cut them out in some way. This dynamic is corrosive, and it doesn't respond well to defensiveness. The most effective approach is radical transparency: share every document, invite them to every attorney meeting, copy them on every communication. Make it impossible to sustain the narrative that something is being hidden. If they remain suspicious despite full access, that's a signal that the issue isn't really about the estate plan.

The Grieving Sibling

Sometimes a sibling's difficult behavior in the estate planning process isn't about money or control at all. It's about grief anticipatory grief over losing a parent, grief over the family changing, grief over a childhood that's being formally closed. Estate planning is a concrete acknowledgment that your parents are mortal, and some siblings find that genuinely destabilizing. Patience matters here. Pushing them through the process before they're emotionally ready tends to produce resistance and resentment. If you can give them space to process while still moving the plan forward, do that.

How to Run a Family Meeting That Produces Decisions

At some point in the estate planning process, a family meeting is probably necessary. Not a casual conversation, a structured gathering where information is shared, decisions are discussed, and everyone has a chance to be heard.

Done well, a family meeting accelerates the process and reduces conflict. Done badly, it becomes the moment everything falls apart. The difference comes down almost entirely to preparation and structure.

Set the agenda in advance. Send it to everyone before the meeting. The agenda should make clear what the meeting is for sharing information about the planning process, not making binding decisions about the estate. Keep the scope narrow. A meeting that tries to resolve every question at once tends to resolve nothing.

Define who is facilitating. Ideally this is a neutral party an elder law attorney, a financial advisor, or a family mediator. If it's one of the siblings, the other siblings must genuinely accept that person as a fair facilitator, which is harder than it sounds. If there's meaningful conflict in the family already, do not attempt to self-facilitate. Bring a professional.

Keep your parents at the center. They should be present if possible and cognitively able. The moment the family starts discussing your parents' wishes and affairs without your parents in the room, it starts to feel like a management meeting, and it often produces decisions that don't reflect what your parents want. Your parent is not a passive subject of this process. They are decision-makers.

Establish ground rules explicitly. One person speaks at a time. No interrupting. No relitigating old family grievances this meeting is about the plan, not about ancient history. Anyone who can't abide by the ground rules gets a break, not an audience.

Document what was discussed and agreed. After the meeting, send a written summary to everyone who was present. Not minutes — a clear, plain-language summary of what was covered and what the next steps are. This eliminates "that's not what I agreed to" conversations later.

> ***Key principle:*** *A family meeting is not a vote. Your parent's estate plan reflects your parent's wishes, not a family consensus. The meeting is for communication and transparency, not for siblings to collectively decide what should happen.*

The Fairness Question and Why Equal Isn't Always Fair

At some point, someone is going to raise the fairness question. It might be about who gets what. It might be about who was named executor or trustee. It might be about why one sibling is receiving more than another.

The first thing to understand is that "fair" and "equal" are not the same thing, and conflating them causes enormous family conflict that is almost entirely unnecessary.

Your parents have the absolute right to distribute their assets however they choose. Full stop. If they want to leave more to a child who provided years of caregiving, that is their right. If they want to skip one child entirely and leave everything to the others, that is their right. If they want to leave a larger share to a grandchild who has a special need, that is their right.

It is not greedy to receive what your parents wanted you to have. It is not unfair for another sibling to receive less if that reflects your parent's genuine wishes. The deceased — or in the planning phase, the living parents already said what they wanted to happen. Their wishes deserve to be honored, not renegotiated by the family after the fact.

That said, decisions that feel arbitrary or unexplained tend to generate more conflict than decisions that come with context. If your parents plans to distribute unequally, encouraging them to have a direct conversation with the family about why while they can still speak for themselves can prevent years of resentment and legal challenges. A parent who explains their reasoning while alive leaves far less room for a disgruntled sibling to claim the plan doesn't reflect their true wishes.

> *The parent's assets are the parents to give. The family doesn't get a vote on that. What the family does get is transparency, and that makes all the difference.*

Handling the Sibling Who Thinks They Should Be in Charge

Naming an executor or trustee is one of the most consequential decisions in an estate plan, and it's also one of the most reliably contentious. Every family seems to have at least one sibling who believes, sincerely and sometimes loudly, that they are the right person for the job.

Sometimes they are. A sibling with a financial background, a track record of good judgment, and a relationship of trust with all parties is a legitimate candidate. But the decision belongs to your parent, and it should be made based on who is best positioned to carry out the role competently and impartially not who wants it most, not who is the oldest, and not who has been applying the most pressure.

The executor's job is not an honor. It is work unglamorous, time-consuming administrative work that involves settling debts, filing tax returns, managing assets during the settlement period, and distributing property according to the plan. Many people who want the title to have not thought seriously about the job.

If a sibling is pushing hard to be named executor or trustee against your parent's inclinations, the right response is to redirect to your parent. This is their decision. The Attorney works for them. If your parent has concerns about a particular sibling's ability to handle the role objectively due to their own financial instability, their conflict with other siblings, or any other factor those concerns are legitimate and should drive the decision.

In genuinely contentious families, naming a professional trustee a trust company or a bank with a trust department rather than a family member can be the cleanest solution. It removes the personal dynamic entirely and puts a neutral, experienced party in charge of administration. It costs more than a family member acting as trustee, but it can easily be worth it in families where any family appointment would generate conflict.

> ***Worth knowing:*** *A corporate trustee or professional executor typically charges 1– 2% of the estate value annually for ongoing trust management, or a flat fee for estate settlement. In families with significant conflict, this cost is often far less than what a legal dispute among siblings would run.*

When a Sibling Is Already Exerting Undue Influence

This is the situation that calls for the most urgent attention, and the one family are most reluctant to name directly. Undue influence happens when someone often a sibling who has positioned themselves as the primary caregiver or the parent's closest confidant begins using that access and trust to shape the estate plan in their own favor. It can happen gradually and without obvious malice. The sibling who drives every appointment starts steering the conversation with the attorney. The sibling who manages the finances starts making decisions that favor themselves. The sibling who controls access to the parent starts limiting what other family members know.

The warning signs are worth knowing:

Your parent's expressed wishes seem to have changed significantly recently, in ways that benefit one person disproportionately. Your parents seem reluctant to speak freely when a particular person is present. A sibling has taken over financial management in ways that aren't transparent to the rest of the family. Documents have been signed without other family members' knowledge. Your parents seem confused about decisions they've supposedly made.

If you see multiple signs of this, the situation calls for direct action rather than a family meeting. An elder law attorney should be engaged independently — not the one already working with the family if that relationship has been compromised. A geriatric care manager or physician can assess your parent's cognitive state and document their capacity. In serious cases, Adult Protective Services can be contacted.

This is not a conversation to have with the suspected sibling first. If undue influence is occurring, alerting the person involved gives them the opportunity to cover their tracks or further isolate your parents. Act through legal and medical channels, not through a family confrontation.

Chapter 12 covers elder financial fraud in full, including when the threat comes from inside the family. If you have genuine concerns about exploitation, go there next.

The Caregiver Contribution Problem

One of the most common and genuinely difficult equity questions in estate planning involves the sibling who has provided significant caregiving.

One child lives nearby and has spent years driving to doctor's appointments, managing medications, handling finances, being available for every emergency. The other children live elsewhere and visit occasionally. When the estate plan leaves equal shares to everyone, the caregiving sibling may feel that years of sacrifice real sacrifice, in time, career impact, and personal cost have been ignored.

When the estate plan leaves a larger share to the caregiving sibling, the other siblings may feel blindsided or cheated, particularly if the decision wasn't discussed openly.

There are a few ways to handle this that tend to produce less conflict than others.

The cleanest approach is for your parents to address it directly and while they're alive. If they want to compensate a caregiving child through the estate plan, saying so explicitly to all the children, in their own words takes the sting out of the discovery after death. It's harder to contest a decision you heard your parents make in person.

Another approach is a formal caregiver agreement a legal document that establishes compensation for caregiving services provided, paid out during the parent's lifetime rather than through the estate. This separates the compensation from the inheritance entirely, which simplifies the estate distribution and reduces the grounds for sibling resentment.

What doesn't work well is leaving the inequality in the estate plan without any explanation, discovered only after the parent dies. That's the scenario most likely to produce legal challenges and permanent family fractures.

When a Sibling Has Borrowed Money and Never Paid It Back

This one comes up more often than most families want to admit. A sibling has received loans from the parents over the years sometimes substantial ones that were never repaid. The estate plan is now being set up, and the question becomes: does that history affect what they receive?

The answer depends entirely on what your parents want. Some parents want those loans treated as advances on inheritance and deducted from that sibling's share. Others have already forgiven the debt mentally and want equal distribution regardless. Either position is legitimate. What creates problems is when the intent is unclear.

If your parents want loans treated as advances, that needs to be documented in the estate plan explicitly. The amount, the intent, and the mechanism for accounting for it should all be addressed in writing with the attorney. A vague reference to "make sure everyone is treated fairly" in conversation is not the same as a legal provision.

If your parents have forgiven the debt and want equal distribution anyway, that's their right but the other siblings deserve to know that this is a considered decision, not an oversight. Discovering after death that a sibling received equal inheritance despite years of unpaid loans and that this was your parent's deliberate choice lands differently than suspecting the sibling somehow got away with something.

Transparency, again, is the thing that keeps these situations from becoming catastrophic.

The Role of the Adult Child Who Initiated This

If you're the one who got this process started who raised the conversation, pushed for the attorney meeting, did the research you may find yourself in an awkward position with your siblings. Even when your motivations are completely protective, the fact that you initiated things can make you look like you're managing the process for your own benefit.

The best way to manage this perception is to be consistently and genuinely transparent. Share information freely. Include siblings in conversations unless there's a specific reason not to. Avoid positioning yourself as the gatekeeper between your parents and the rest of the family.

And be honest with yourself about your own interests. You're human. You may have preferences about how the estate is distributed or who serves as executor. Those preferences are not disqualifying, but they do mean you need to be careful about the line between advocating for your parents' wishes and advocating for your own.

When in doubt, let the attorney lead. A good elder law attorney keeps your parent at the center of every decision and makes it structurally difficult for any one family member including you to unduly shape the outcome. That's not a limitation. That's the system working correctly.

Family Harmony Is Worth Planning For

The families that come through this process intact that settle an estate without a lawsuit, without a sibling feud, without years of silence at holidays, are not families without conflict.

They're families where someone took the time to manage the process well. Transparent communication. A clearly documented plan that reflects the parent's genuine wishes. Siblings who felt heard even when they didn't get exactly what they wanted.

That doesn't happen by accident. It happens because someone often the person holding this book took it seriously enough to do the work.

The document side of estate planning is the easy part. Attorneys know how to draft wills and trusts. The hard part is the human side: the conversations, the family dynamics, the old grievances that estate planning has a way of surfacing. This chapter has been about that hard part.

Part Two of this book turns to the practical side the documents themselves, explained in plain language, so you know exactly what your parents needs and why. Chapter 4 starts with the question most families get wrong: the difference between a will and a living trust, and why that difference matters far more than most people realize.

PART TWO: UNDERSTANDING WHAT YOUR PARENT ACTUALLY NEEDS

The Documents, the Decisions, and the Differences That Matter

CHAPTER 4

Will vs. Living Trust: What Nobody Explains Clearly

Most families know they need "something." They're less clear on what that something is or why the difference between a will and a living trust matters as much as it does. By the end of this chapter, that confusion is gone.

The Misconception That Costs Families the Most

Here is the single most expensive misunderstanding in estate planning: a will keeps your estate out of probate.

It does not. A will goes through probate. That is, in fact, what a will is designed to do — it is a set of instructions for the probate court to follow. The court reads the will, validates it, supervises the distribution of assets, and closes the estate. That process takes time, costs money, and is open to the public. Anyone can walk into a courthouse and read your parent's will after they die.

A living trust, when properly set up and funded, bypasses the probate court entirely. Assets held in the trust transfer directly to beneficiaries according to the trust's instructions, without court involvement, without public disclosure, and typically in a matter of weeks rather than months or years.

These are not slightly different versions of the same thing. They are fundamentally different tools with fundamentally different outcomes. And yet millions of families treat them as interchangeable, assume the will alone is sufficient, and discover the difference at the worst possible time — when a parent has just died and someone must deliver the news that the estate is going to be tied up in probate for the next year and a half.

> *A will tells the probate court what your parent wanted. A living trust makes the probate court unnecessary.*

What Probate Actually Is and Why It Matters

Probate is the legal process by which a deceased person's estate is settled under court supervision. It involves validating the will, inventorying assets, notifying creditors, paying debts and taxes, and ultimately distributing what's left to the beneficiaries named in the will.

In concept, it's a consumer protection mechanism a way of ensuring that debts are paid and that assets go to the right people. In practice, for most families, it is an expensive, slow, and unnecessarily public process that adds real cost and real delay to what is already an emotionally difficult time.

Here is what probate typically involves in concrete terms:

Time. Probate takes a minimum of several months in most states and commonly runs 12 to 24 months for estates of any complexity. During this period, assets are frozen. The family cannot sell the house, cannot access bank accounts held solely in the deceased's name, cannot distribute personal property. Everything waits on the court.

Cost. Attorney fees, executor fees, court filing fees, appraisal costs, and other administrative expenses typically consume 3 to 8 percent of the gross estate value not the net value after debts, but the gross value before. On a $500,000 estate, that's

$15,000 to $40,000 in fees. On a modest estate with a house worth $300,000 and

$50,000 in savings, families are sometimes shocked to find that a significant portion of what their parent worked a lifetime to accumulate goes to the process of distributing it.

Public exposure. Everything filed in probate becomes part of the public record. The value of the estate, the names of the beneficiaries, the specific assets involved, any disputes that arise, all of it is accessible to anyone who wants to look. This matters more than most families initially realize. It attracts creditors. It invites challenges from distant relatives or ex-spouses.

And it exposes the family's financial situation at a moment of vulnerability.

Multi-state complexity. If your parents own real property in more than one state, a vacation home, a rental property, land the estate may have to go through probate in each state where real property is located. Each state has its own rules, its own timeline, and its own costs. A living trust holds property in all states and distributes it through one document, under one set of instructions, without triggering multiple probate proceedings.

> ***Real numbers:*** *The American Bar Association estimates that probate costs the average estate 3–8% of its gross value. For a $400,000 estate, that's between $12,000 and $32,000, money that a properly funded living trust would have kept in the family.*

What a WILL Actually Does

A will, formally, a Last Will and Testament is a legal document in which your parent specifies how they want their assets distributed after death, names an executor to carry out those instructions, and (if applicable) designates guardians for minor children.

It is a necessary document. Every adult should have one. But it is not sufficient on its own for most families and understanding what it does and does not cover is essential.

A will covers assets that are owned solely in your parent's name and have no other mechanism for transfer. It does not cover assets that have named beneficiaries life insurance policies, retirement accounts, and bank accounts with payable-on-death designations pass directly to the named beneficiary regardless of what the will says. It does not cover assets held in joint tenancy with right of survivorship, which pass automatically to the surviving owner. And it does not cover anything already held in a trust.

This means the will's actual reach is often narrower than families expect. If your parent's house is titled solely in their name, the will governs it — and it goes through probate. If their retirement accounts have an outdated beneficiary designation naming a deceased spouse, the will doesn't fix that. Each asset type has its own transfer mechanism, and the will only controls a subset of them.

A will also takes effect only at death. It says nothing about who manages your parent's affairs if they become incapacitated. For that, you need a durable power of attorney and healthcare directive — documents covered in Chapter 5.

What a Living Trust Actually Is

A revocable living trust is a legal entity that holds assets during your parent's lifetime and distributes them after death according to the trust's instructions without court involvement.

Here's the simplest way to understand it: your parents create trust, names themselves as the initial trustee, and retains complete control over everything in it. They can add assets, remove assets, change the terms, or revoke the trust entirely at any point during their lifetime. Nothing changes about how they use or manage their property. Trust is essentially invisible during their lifetime.

When they die or if they become incapacitated the successor trustee named steps in and takes over. That successor trustee has the legal authority to manage, distribute, or sell assets according to the trust's instructions, without going to court, without waiting for probate, and without any public process.

That transition from your parents managing their own assets to the successor trustee managing them can happen in days rather than the months or years probate requires. Bills keep getting paid. The house doesn't sit frozen while the court processes paperwork. The family can focus on grief rather than legal logistics.

Trust also covers incapacity, which a will does not. If your parent has a stroke or develops dementia and can no longer manage their finances, the successor trustee steps in under the trust's terms, no court petition required, no conservatorship proceeding, no judge deciding who gets control. The plan your parent set up in advance governs exactly what happens.

The One Thing That Makes a Living Trust Worthless

A living trust that hasn't been funded is a legal document with no practical effect.

Funding the trust means retitling assets into the trust's name. The house, bank accounts, investment accounts, and other assets need to be legally transferred from your parent's individual name into the trust. An asset that remains in your parent's individual name at death goes through probate regardless of what the trust says because the trust doesn't own it.

This is where a surprising number of estate plans fall apart. The attorney drafts a perfectly good trust document. Your parents signs it. Everyone feels like the job is done. And then nobody transfers the assets into the trust. Years later, your parents die. The family assumes the trust will handle everything. And then they find out the house is still titled in your parent's name, not the trust's name, and they're going through probate anyway.

Funding a trust requires real work: deeds need to be redrawn and recorded for real estate, financial institutions need to be contacted to retitle accounts, and the trust needs to be listed as beneficiary or owner on the appropriate assets. It is not complicated, but it requires follow-through. Many estate planning attorneys handle funding as part of their engagement. If yours does not, that's something to clarify before you leave the office.

Chapter 15 walks through the funding process step by step, including which assets should go into the trust and which should not.

> ***Critical point:*** *An unfunded trust is one of the most common and most avoidable estate planning failures. Ask your attorney directly: what is your process for making sure the trust is funded before we're done?*

Will vs. Living Trust: The Comparison at a Glance

The table below summarizes the core differences. Take a moment with it, because these distinctions drive almost every decision in the chapters that follow.

	Last Will & Testament	Revocable Living Trust
Goes through probate?	Yes — always	No bypasses probate entirely when funded

The pattern is clear. A will is simpler and cheaper to create. A living trust costs more to establish but saves significantly more in time, money, and family stress on the back end. For families with a home, meaningful savings, or any complexity at all, the living trust is almost always the right foundation.

Do You Still Need a Will If You Have a Living Trust?

Yes. Even with a comprehensive living trust, every person should have a will. Here's why.

Public record?	Yes — anyone can access it	No — entirely private
Covers incapacity?	No — only takes effect at death	Yes — successor trustee steps in immediately

Cost to establish	Lower upfront ($300–$1,000)	Higher upfront ($1,500–$3,500+)
Cost to settle estate	High — probate fees often 3–8% of estate	Low — no probate required
Time to distribute assets	6 months to 2+ years	Weeks to a few months
Covers assets in multiple states?	No — separate probate required in each state	Yes — one trust covers all states
Can be contested?	Yes — relatively easier to challenge	Harder to contest — higher legal bar

No matter how carefully a trust is funded, it is almost impossible to guarantee that every asset is captured. A small bank account opened after the trust was established. A personal injury settlement. A tax refund. Any asset that ends up in your parent's name at death and isn't in the trust will need somewhere to go and a will provides that direction.

The will that accompanies a living trust is called a pour-over will. It essentially says: anything I own at death that isn't already in my trust goes into my trust at that point, to be distributed according to the trust's terms. It's a catch-all. Assets that pour over through the will do go through probate, but if the trust is properly funded, those assets should be minimal. The pour-over will handle the edges; the trust handles the substance.

A will also does things a trust cannot. It is called a guardian for minor children. It can express wishes about personal property that are too specific for a trust document. It can include a statement of final wishes, values, or instructions that the trust isn't the right vehicle for.

The TRUST and the WILL work together. They are not alternatives, they are complements. Any estate plan built on just one of them is incomplete.

When a WILL Alone Might Be Sufficient

There are situations where a simpler plan, a will rather than a full trust is genuinely adequate. Knowing when that's the case saves money and unnecessary complexity.

A will-only plan may be sufficient when the estate is small enough to fall below the state's probate threshold. Many states have simplified probate procedures for small estates typically under $100,000 to $200,000 depending on the state. If your parent's estate falls into that range and consists primarily of assets with named beneficiaries or joint ownership, the probate process may be straightforward enough that full trust isn't warranted.

It may also be sufficient when your parents' primary assets already bypass probate through other mechanisms. A home held in joint tenancy with a surviving spouse, retirement accounts and life insurance with up-to-date beneficiary designations, and bank accounts with payable-on-death designations can leave very little subject to probate even without a trust.

What it is not sufficient for: any estate that includes real property titled solely in your parent's name, any estate that involves real property in multiple states, any situation involving a blended family, any parent with a child who has addiction or financial management issues, or any estate large enough that probate fees represent a meaningful loss.

What Families Find Out Too Late

The conversations that never should have had to happen go something like this: a parent dies. The adult children assume the estate will be handled quickly. Then they learn the house — the primary asset, the one thing their parent worked for 35 years — is titled solely in the deceased's name with no trust, no joint ownership, no other mechanism to avoid probate.

So they hire a probate attorney. They file the will. They wait. Six months in, there's a creditor claim. Eight months in, a distant relative surfaces with a question about the will's validity. Fourteen months in, the house finally sells, and after probate fees and legal costs, the net amount that reaches the family is meaningfully less than what their parent left.

None of that was inevitable. A properly funded living trust would have transferred the house to the beneficiaries within weeks of death, with no court involvement, no creditor window, no public record, and no attorney fees beyond a modest trust administration cost.

This is not a scare story. It is a pattern, repeated in families every single day, simply because the difference between a will and a living trust wasn't explained clearly enough, soon enough.

Now you know the difference. The question is what to do with that knowledge.

The Foundation Is the Trust

For most families with aging parents, the foundation of the estate plan is a revocable living trust, supported by a pour-over will, a durable power of attorney, a healthcare directive, and a HIPAA authorization. These five documents work together to cover every major scenario: death, incapacity, medical decisions, and financial management.

Chapter 5 walks through each of those five documents in detail — what each one does, who needs to be named in it, and what happens without it. By the end of that chapter, you'll have a complete picture of what your parent's plan needs to include and why.

CHAPTER 5

The Five Documents That Protect Everything

Most families know they need "something" in place. What they don't always know is that "something" is five specific documents, each covering a different scenario, and missing even one of them leaves a real gap. This chapter explains what each document does, who needs to be named in it, and what happens to your family without it.

Why Five Documents and Not One

There is no single document that handles everything. This is one of the most common false assumptions families make, and it costs them.

A living trust handles asset distribution and management during incapacity but only for assets held in the trust, and only for financial matters. It says nothing about medical decisions. A will covers assets that fall outside the trust, names guardians for minor children, and provides the court with instructions but it only takes effect at death and does nothing for incapacity. A durable power of attorney authorizes someone to manage finances if your parent can't, but it doesn't make medical decisions. A healthcare directive covers medical decisions but not finances. And a HIPAA authorization is the one document without which none of the others function as

intended, because without it, no one can legally discuss their parents' medical situation with their doctors.

Each document fills a specific gap. Together, they form a complete plan. Missing one means that some scenario incapacity, a medical emergency, a financial crisis during illness lands on your family without any legal framework to handle it.

Here is each document, explained plainly.

DOCUMENT 1

Revocable Living Trust

The foundation of the estate plan

What it does

A revocable living trust is a legal entity your parent creates to hold their assets during their lifetime and distribute them after death — without going through probate. As covered in Chapter 4, your parents serve as their own trustee while they're alive and

capable, retaining full control over everything in the trust. When they die or become incapacitated, a successor trustee steps in and manages or distributes the assets according to the trust's instructions.

The trust covers the full scope of your parent's financial life: their home, bank accounts, investment accounts, business interests, and other significant assets. It can also include provisions for incapacity specifying exactly how assets should be managed if your parents can no longer manage them personally, without requiring a court to appoint anyone or supervise the process.

Who needs to be named

Three roles need to be filled in every living trust. The grantor is your parent the person creating the trust. The trustee is the person managing the trust; initially this is your parents themselves. The successor trustee is the person who takes over when your parent can no longer serve, this is one of the most important appointments in the entire plan.

Choosing a successor trustee deserves serious thought. This person will have real authority over real assets at a moment of family stress. They need to be trustworthy, organized, capable of handling financial and legal tasks, and able to deal with financial institutions, attorneys, and sometimes contentious family members. Being a good person is necessary but not sufficient. Being capable and available is equally important.

Most trusts also name a backup successor trustee in case the first choice is unable or unwilling to serve when the time comes.

What happens without it

Assets in your parent's name go through probate. The process is public, slow, and expensive. If your parent becomes incapacitated without a trust, the family may need to go to court for a conservatorship to manage their finances, a process that costs thousands of dollars and puts a judge, rather than your parent's chosen successor, in charge.

> ***Common mistake:*** *Signing the trust document but never funding it. An unfunded trust provides zero probate protection. Every asset must be retitled into the trust's name for the trust to work. See Chapter 15 for the complete funding walkthrough.*

DOCUMENT 2

Last Will and Testament

The safety net and the catch-all

What it does

Even with a comprehensive living trust, your parents need a will. As discussed in Chapter 4, a pour-over will serves as the catch-all for any assets that weren't transferred into the trust during your parent's lifetime. At death, those stray assets "pour over" into the trust and are distributed according to its terms.

The will also does things the trust cannot. It is called a guardian for any minor children or grandchildren your parents may be responsible for. It can address specific personal property, who gets the watch, the furniture, the car in a way that a trust document isn't really designed for. And it gives your parents a place to express final wishes, values, and instructions that don't fit neatly into legal trust language.

Who needs to be named

The executor is the person responsible for carrying out the will's instructions and managing the probate process for any assets that go through it. In a trust-based plan, the executor's role is usually limited because most assets are held in the trust. But the role still exists and still needs to be filled by someone capable and trustworthy.

If your parent has minor children or grandchildren in their care, a guardian needs to be named. This is one of the most personal and consequential appointments in any estate plan. It should reflect genuine consideration of who is best positioned to raise those children, not just who is the obvious choice by default.

What happens without it

Any asset not held in the trust and not transferred by beneficiary designation or joint ownership has no direction. State intestacy laws determine where it goes, which may not reflect your parent's wishes. And if your parent is responsible for minor children with no guardian named, a court appoints one.

> ***Worth noting:*** *A will that hasn't been updated in more than five years should be reviewed. Life changes — divorce, death of a named executor, new grandchildren, changed relationships — can make an old will not just outdated but actively counterproductive.*

DOCUMENT 3

Durable Power of Attorney

For finances when your parent can no longer manage

What it does

A durable power of attorney — sometimes called a financial power of attorney authorizes a designated person (the agent) to make financial decisions on your parent's behalf if they become incapacitated. The word "durable" is critical: it means the document remains in effect even if your parent loses mental capacity. A regular power of attorney terminates the moment the person becomes incapacitated, which is precisely when you need it most. The durable version is designed to survive incapacity. The scope of authority a DPOA grants can be broad or narrow. A broad DPOA authorizes the agent to manage bank accounts, pay bills, handle investments, file taxes, manage real estate, and conduct essentially any financial transaction your parent could conduct themselves. A limited DPOA restricts authority to specific transactions or a specific period.

For most aging parents, a broad durable power of attorney is appropriate. The agent needs enough authority to manage the full scope of the parent's financial life during an extended illness or period of incapacity.

Who needs to be named

The agent sometimes called the attorney. is the person with authority to act under the DPOA. This is arguably the most trust-sensitive appointment in the entire estate plan. The agent has real, immediate authority over real assets. Unlike a trustee's authority, which is governed by trust terms and fiduciary duties with meaningful legal accountability, a DPOA agent's authority is broad, and their accountability is largely practical rather than legal.

Choose this person carefully. The qualities that matter most are financial competence, scrupulous honesty, availability, and the ability to navigate financial institutions and keep records. Being a loving family member is not sufficient qualification on its own. A history of financial instability, substance issues, or conflict with other family members is disqualifying.

Name a backup agent. If the primary agent is unavailable when needed due to their own illness, death, or an unwillingness to serve the backup steps in without requiring a new document.

What happens without it

If your parent becomes incapacitated with no DPOA in place, someone — almost certainly a family member — must petition a court for a conservatorship or guardianship to manage your parent's finances. This process typically costs $3,000 to
$10,000 or more in legal fees, takes months, requires ongoing court supervision, and puts a judge in control of who gets that authority. It's expensive, slow, and strips your parent of the ability to choose who manages their affairs.

> **Important distinction:** A living trust handles assets held in the trust. A durable power of attorney handles everything else — assets not yet in the trust, government benefits, tax filings, leases, and other financial matters that exist outside the trust's reach. Both documents are needed. Neither one alone is sufficient.

DOCUMENT 4

Healthcare Directive / Living Will

For medical decisions when your parent cannot speak for themselves

What it does

A healthcare directive is sometimes called a living will, an advanced directive, or a healthcare proxy depending on the state does two related things. First, it designates a healthcare agent (sometimes called a healthcare proxy or medical power of attorney) who has the legal authority to make medical decisions on your parent's behalf if they cannot make those decisions themselves. Second, it documents your parents' actual wishes about specific medical situations like support, resuscitation, artificial nutrition, and other interventions so that those wishes guide decisions even if the healthcare agent isn't immediately reachable.

Without a healthcare directive, medical staff default to next of kin a designation that varies by state and may not reflect who your parents would have chosen. In families with complicated dynamics, this can mean the person making medical decisions is not the person your parents trusted most, and it can mean that siblings with different views on end-of-life care are suddenly in conflict during a medical crisis.

A healthcare directive eliminates that ambiguity. Your parents choose who speaks for them. Your parents' wishes about specific interventions are documented. Medical staff have clear legal authority to follow those instructions.

Who needs to be named

The healthcare agent is the person authorized to make medical decisions. This person needs to be someone who genuinely understands your parent's values and wishes, can communicate clearly under pressure with medical staff, and can make difficult decisions in difficult moments without becoming paralyzed by grief or family conflict.

This is not necessarily the same person as the financial power of attorney agent or the successor trustee. Medical decision-making requires a different set of qualities than financial management. Your parent should think about who they want in that room making those calls — not just who is the most organized or most financially capable.

Name a backup healthcare agent. Medical crises don't wait for convenient timing, and the primary agent may not be immediately available.

The specific wishes your parent needs to document

The directive should address, at minimum: cardiopulmonary resuscitation (CPR) preferences, mechanical ventilation, artificial nutrition and hydration, comfort care versus aggressive treatment preferences, and organ donation wishes. These are the decisions that medical staff most commonly face with incapacitated patients, and they are the decisions that generate the most family conflict when there is no documented guidance.

The conversation about these specific wishes is hard. It is also one of the most loving things a family can do together. Giving your parents the chance to say, clearly and on the record, what they would and would not want at the end of their life is a profound act of respect.

What happens without it

Medical staff make decisions based on default protocols and next-of-kin hierarchy. Family members who disagree with those decisions have limited recourse. In the worst cases, siblings end up in court seeking guardianship specifically to gain medical decision-making authority during an active medical crisis, under enormous emotional pressure.

> ***State variation:*** *Healthcare directive requirements vary significantly by state — the document name, the witnessing requirements, and even what decisions can be pre-authorized differ. An elder law attorney can ensure your parent's directive meets the specific requirements of their state.*

DOCUMENT 5

HIPAA Authorization

So you can talk to their doctors

What it does

The Health Insurance Portability and Accountability Act — HIPAA — protects the privacy of medical information. That protection is genuinely important. It also means that without explicit written authorization from your parent, their doctors, hospitals, and insurers cannot legally discuss their medical situation with anyone — including their adult children.

A HIPAA authorization is a document in which your parent explicitly designates who may receive their medical information. It is not a decision-making document — it does not authorize anyone to make medical decisions, which is what the healthcare directive does. It simply authorizes the flow of information to specific people.

Without it, even the most carefully named healthcare agent may find themselves unable to get basic information from a hospital — not because the hospital is being obstructionist, but because their hands are legally tied. The HIPAA authorization is what unlocks the conversation.

Who needs to be named

Anyone your parent wants to be able to discuss their medical information should be named. This typically includes the healthcare agent, the successor trustee, and any adult children who may be involved in care decisions, even if they're not the primary decision-maker. It can also include a primary care physician who coordinates care across providers, or other trusted individuals. The HIPAA authorization and the healthcare directive are often prepared together by the estate planning attorney, since the same people are typically named in both. But they serve different functions and both need to exist.

What happens without it

Family members who are not named on a HIPAA authorization can be legally locked out of medical conversations even in crisis situations. An adult child trying to help coordinate a parent's care from across the country may find they cannot get any information from the hospital treating their parent. A healthcare agent who cannot get information about the parent's condition cannot make informed decisions on their behalf.

This is the shortest and simplest of the five documents. It is also the one most overlooked. It takes minutes to complete and can make an enormous practical difference.

> ***Do not skip this one:*** *Families who have every other document in place sometimes assume the HIPAA authorization is a formality. It is not. Without it, the other documents cannot function as intended in a medical setting.*

How the Five Documents Work Together

Each document covers a specific gap. Together, they cover every significant scenario your family is likely to face.

When your parents are alive and well, the living trust quietly holds their assets and the other documents sit in a folder, ready but unused. Nothing changes about how your parent lives or manages their affairs.

When your parent becomes incapacitated — through illness, accident, or cognitive decline — three documents activate immediately. The successor trustee takes over management of trust assets. The durable power of attorney agent manages financial matters outside the trust. The healthcare directive and healthcare agent govern medical decisions. The HIPAA authorization allows everyone who needs information to get it. No court involvement. No legal proceedings. No gap in coverage.

When your parents die, the living trust distributes assets directly to beneficiaries without probate. The pour-over will capture anything that fell outside the trust. The executor manages the limited probate process for those stray assets.

The plan works because each document is handed off cleanly to the next. Remove one and you introduce a gap — a scenario where there's no legal framework, and someone must either improvise or go to court.

> *The goal of the five-document plan is that no matter what happens — illness, incapacity, or death — there is always a clear, legally sound answer to the question: who is in charge, and what do they do next?*

Turning Knowledge into Action

If your parents have none of these documents, the priority order is straightforward. Start with the healthcare directive and HIPAA authorization these are the most immediately relevant if there's any health uncertainty, and they are the fastest to complete. Add the durable power of attorney. Then work with an elder law attorney to draft the living trust and pour-over will, and begin the funding process.

If your parents have some of these documents but not all, identify the gaps and fill them. A will without a trust, a trust without a DPOA, a healthcare directive without a HIPAA authorization, each partial plan has a specific vulnerability that a specific document addresses.

If your parent has all five documents but they haven't been reviewed recently, Chapter 18 covers when and how to update an estate plan. A document that doesn't reflect your parent's current assets, relationships, and wishes can be as problematic as no document at all.

CHAPTER 6

What Happens When There's No Plan and a Crisis Hits

Abstract warnings about the importance of estate planning only go so far. This chapter makes the consequences concrete — real scenarios, real costs, real families, and the decisions that changed everything.

When the Theoretical Becomes Real

Most people understand, in an abstract way, that not having an estate plan is a problem. They've heard the word probate. They know they should have a will. They've nodded along when someone mentioned the power of attorney.

And then nothing happens. Because understanding something in the abstract is very different from feeling its weight. The urgency never quite materializes until the crisis does.

This chapter is about what the crisis looks like — not hypothetically, but in the specific, concrete, dollars-and-months reality that families encounter when a parent dies or becomes incapacitated without a plan in place. The scenarios that follow represent the real consequences of decisions that felt easy to defer.

Read them not as horror stories but as maps. Each one shows you exactly where the gap in the plan was, what it cost, and what a different decision would have produced.

SCENARIO 1

The House That Took Two Years to Transfer

No living trust. The estate goes through probate. The family waits.

A widowed mother dies at 79. She owned her home outright — paid off, worth approximately $380,000. She had a will, drafted in 2009, leaving everything equally to her three adult children. No living trust. No other planning beyond the will.

Her eldest daughter, named executor, files the will with the probate court six weeks after the funeral. The court validates it and opens the estate. What follows is 22 months of proceedings.

A creditor surfaces with a medical debt from a hospitalization two years prior. The estate cannot distribute assets until the claim is resolved. The house cannot be sold until the court authorizes it. One sibling living out of state grows increasingly frustrated. Tension develops over whether to accept a lower offer to speed things up.

By the time the estate closes, the family has paid $24,000 in probate attorney fees, $3,200 in court costs, and $8,500 in real estate commissions. The house sold for $15,000 less than peak value because the family took a lower offer to end the ordeal. Total loss compared to a clean transfer: approximately $51,000 — not including 22 months of compounding sibling conflict.

A funded living trust would have transferred the house within four to six weeks of death, at a cost of a few hundred dollars in trust administration. The creditor claim would still have needed addressing — but on the family's timeline, not the court's.

> ***The gap:*** *A will does not avoid probate. It is the instruction manual for the probate process. Only a properly funded living trust bypasses probate entirely.*

SCENARIO 2

The Stroke and the Missing Power of Attorney

Incapacity without a DPOA. A family goes to court to manage their own father's finances.

A 74-year-old man suffers a severe stroke. He survives but loses the ability to communicate clearly and cannot manage his finances. His wife died three years earlier. Two adult children, a nearby son who has been helping, and a daughter across the country who has been less involved.

He has a will. He does not have a durable power of attorney.

The son tries to manage his father's accounts by paying bills, handling the mortgage, and dealing with insurance claims. The bank refuses access. Without a DPOA, he has no legal authority over his father's finances. The bank is not being obstructionist. It is following the law.

The son petitions the court for conservatorship. The process requires an attorney, a formal petition, a court-appointed investigator, a hearing before a judge, and ongoing court supervision. The daughter, who disagrees with some of the son's decisions, contests portions of the petition. Eight months have passed.

Legal fees for the conservatorship: $14,200. Annual court supervision: $1,800. The mortgage went 60 days delinquent during the gap, affecting the estate's credit and complicating the eventual home sale.

A durable power of attorney, signed when the father was healthy, would have cost $200 to $400 as part of a basic estate plan. It would have given the son immediate legal authority the day after the stroke no court, no eight-month delay, no mortgage delinquency.

> ***The gap:*** *A living trust handles trust assets during incapacity. A DPOA handles everything else accounts outside the trust, government benefits, tax filings, insurance claims. Both are needed. One without the other leaves a gap that a crisis will find.*

SCENARIO 3

The Medical Crisis and the Family That Couldn't Agree

No healthcare directive. Three siblings. Three different ideas about what their mother would have wanted.

A 71-year-old woman has a major cardiac event and is placed on life support. Her prognosis is poor. No realistic prospect of meaningful recovery. She has a will but no healthcare directive, no healthcare proxy designation, and no documented wishes about end-of-life care.

Two of her three children believe she would not have wanted to be kept on machines indefinitely. The third believes every possible measure should be taken and refuses to consent to any change in treatment.

The hospital's ethics committee convenes. The two siblings seek guardianship for medical decision-making authority. The third retains their own attorney to contest it. Eleven days pass. Their mother remains on life support throughout.

Legal fees across both sides: approximately $22,000. Their mother passes away in a manner that two of her children believed she would have found deeply contrary to her values. The relationship between the two sides of the family does not recover.

A one-page healthcare directive, signed during any estate planning session or routine medical appointment, would have documented her wishes and named the person authorized to enforce them. The 11-day standoff, the $22,000 in legal fees, and the permanent family fracture were all avoidable.

> **The gap:** A healthcare directive doesn't make the decision — it records your parent's decision in advance, so no one else must make it under pressure, without information, and in open disagreement.

SCENARIO 4

The Blended Family and the Unintended Disinheritance

No updated estate plan after remarriage. The biological children nearly lose everything.

A widower remarries at 68. He has two biological children from his first marriage. His new wife has no children. His existing will leaves everything to his first wife — now deceased — with his two children as alternates. He intends to update the will after the remarriage. He dies of a heart attack 14 months later, before he gets around to it.

Under his state's law, the new spouse is entitled to an elective share of roughly one- third of the estate regardless of the will. The rest passes to the biological children as named alternates. But the house is titled solely in his name, owned for 22 years, the one his children grew up in enters probate. His wife has the legal right to remain under spousal protection laws, but she doesn't own it. His children inherit a house they can't easily sell while their stepmother lives in it. She has limited resources of her own. Nobody wins. The law resolved the situation in a way he never intended.

One post-remarriage conversation with an estate planning attorney one that took the blended family situation seriously would have clarified every expectation, set up the right trust structure, and protected both his wife and his children according to his actual wishes.

SCENARIO 5

The Sibling Who Emptied the Accounts

No trust, no oversight structure. A vulnerable parent. A trusted child with unchecked access.

An 82-year-old woman with early-stage dementia lives with her youngest son, who manages her finances. She has a will to leave her estate equally to her three children. No trust. No formal oversight structure for her financial management.

Over 18 months, the youngest son transfers approximately $190,000 from her accounts into his own through a series of transactions characterized as gifts, loans, and payment for caregiving services. By the time the other two siblings become aware and retain an attorney, their mother has passed.

The estate that should have funded equal shares for three beneficiaries has been largely depleted. Recovery requires suing their own brother — a case that takes three years, costs $38,000 in legal fees, and yields a fraction of what was taken.

A revocable living trust with co-trustee requirements and two signatures required for significant transactions would have made the transfers structurally impossible. Regular accountings built into the trust terms would have made any irregularities visible early. The oversight structure would have been both deterrent and backstop.

The Real Costs at a Glance

These scenarios represent the most common categories of crisis that arise from inadequate estate planning. The financial costs are consistent with what families encounter in practice.

Situation	Without a plan	With a plan
No living trust — probate required	$15,000–$51,000+ in fees	$1,500–$3,500 trust setup
No DPOA — conservatorship required	$10,000–$20,000+ in legal fees	$200–$400 as part of estate plan
No healthcare directive — family conflict	$15,000–$30,000 in legal fees	One-page document, minimal cost
No updated plan after remarriage	Unintended distribution, disputes	One attorney meeting post-remarriage
No oversight structure — exploitation	$38,000+ in litigation, partial recovery	Trust with co-trustee provisions

The pattern holds every time. Planning costs hundreds to a few thousand dollars and a few hours with an attorney. Not planning costs tens of thousands of dollars, months or years of legal proceedings, and family relationships that often don't survive the process intact.

> *Every family that has been through one of these situations will tell you the same thing: they wish someone had pushed harder, sooner, to get the documents in place. Nobody ever wishes they planned too early.*

The Conservatorship Process, Explained

Because it comes up in so many crisis scenarios and is so poorly understood, it's worth spending a moment on what conservatorship involves beyond the dollar figures.

When an adult becomes incapacitated without the power of attorney in place, someone who wants to legally help them must petition a court to be appointed as their conservator (finances) or guardian (personal and medical decisions). Some states use these terms interchangeably; the process is essentially the same. A petition is filed. The court appoints an investigator to assess the incapacitated person's situation. A hearing is scheduled. All interested parties are notified and may participate. A judge issued an appointment order. The appointed person then operates under ongoing court supervision, filing annual accountings, seeking court approval for significant transactions, and justifying their decisions on an ongoing basis.

The process is designed to protect vulnerable adults from exploitation, and that purpose is legitimate. But for families dealing with a sick or incapacitated parent, it feels exactly like what it is: a court inserting itself into deep personal decisions, at significant expense, because no one made those decisions in advance when it was easy to do so.

A durable power of attorney and healthcare directive, signed when your parent was fully capable, make this process unnecessary. The appointments your parents made are honored. No court. No legal fees. No supervision. The plan your parents built governs.

The Cost That Doesn't Show Up in Legal Bills

Every scenario in this chapter has a dollar figure attached. But there's a cost that never appears in any invoice, and it's often the one family feels most acutely.

When estate planning fails, the family is dealing with grief, fear, or the exhaustion of caregiving at the exact same moment they're navigating legal and financial complexity they were never prepared for. These things happen simultaneously. There is no grace period where the legal situation pauses while the family catches its breath.

The sibling conflicts that emerge during these crises often outlast the legal resolution by years. Families that were close before a parent's death sometimes stop speaking in the aftermath of a contested estate not because they were fundamentally incompatible, but because the absence of a clear plan forced them into adversarial positions during the worst time of their lives.

A clear, documented estate plan doesn't guarantee family harmony. But it removes the largest structural sources of conflict. When everyone knows what the plan is, when the legal authority is clearly established, and when the plan reflects what the parent wanted, the space for destructive conflict shrinks dramatically.

The families that come through this process with relationships intact are almost always the families who planned.

From Understanding to Action

Six chapters in, the picture is complete. You understand why the conversation is hard, how to have it, how to navigate the sibling dynamics, what the five essential documents are and what each one does, and what happens to real families when those documents aren't in place.

Part Three moves into the financial realities beneath the planning how to take inventory of what your parents owns, how to protect the family home, what long- term care costs, and the tax and beneficiary mistakes that quietly cost heirs thousands of dollars.

Chapter 7 starts with the most practical first step: figuring out what your parents have.

PART THREE: THE MONEY REALITY

Assets, Taxes, Long-Term Care, and What Your Parent Hasn't Told You

CHAPTER 7

Taking Inventory: Finding What Your Parent Owns

Before you can protect anything, you must know what's there. Most families are surprised by what they find and by what they can't find. This chapter walks through how to build a complete picture of your parent's financial life, even when the records are scattered, incomplete, or never discussed.

The Problem with "*I Think They Have Something*"

This is where most families start: a vague sense that there is a house, probably some savings, maybe a life insurance policy from years ago, and some retirement account somewhere. Beyond that, details get fuzzy.

That fuzziness is not unusual. A lot of aging parents come from a generation that treated finances as deeply private. They didn't discuss account balances with their children. They paid bills on their own terms. They managed their affairs without input and without transparency, and they saw nothing wrong with that because for most of their lives, it worked fine.

The problem arrives when their children suddenly need to manage those affairs during an illness, after a death, in the middle of a financial crisis and have no idea where anything is. Bank accounts at institutions they've never heard of. A life insurance policy purchased in 1987 with a company that has since merged twice. A retirement account from a job ended 20 years ago that nobody thought to roll over. Real estate in another state. A safe deposit box whose location nobody knows.

Finding these things under normal circumstances takes effort. Finding them under crisis circumstances, on a deadline, while also dealing with grief or a medical emergency, is genuinely difficult and sometimes results in assets being missed entirely.

The inventory conversation done now, while your parents are healthy and able to walk you through everything is one of the most practical gifts you can give your future self and your family.

> *An estate plan without a complete asset inventory is a map with half the territory missing. The documents tell you what to do. The inventory tells you what you're doing it with.*

How to Have the Inventory Conversation

This conversation is different from the estate planning conversation in one important way: it's less emotionally charged. You're not asking about death or control or family dynamics. You're asking practical questions about practical things. Most parents find this easier to engage with than the broader estate planning discussion.

The framing that works best centers on helping rather than planning. Something like: "I just want to make sure I'd know what to do and where to find things if I ever needed to help you. Can we put together a simple list?" That's not threatening. It's useful.

Go through its category-by-category real estate, bank accounts, investments, retirement accounts, insurance, digital accounts. Don't try to do it all in one sitting. Schedule it across two or three conversations if your parent has a complex financial life, or if the detailed work is tiring for them.

And write it down. Not in your head, not in a text message in a format that can be found, shared with the attorney, and updated as things change.

> ***Practical tip:*** *Offer to do the writing yourself while your parents talks. Handing someone a form to fill out can feel like homework. Sitting with them while you take notes feels like a conversation.*

The Eight Categories to Cover

A complete asset inventory covers eight distinct categories. Each has its own transfer mechanism, its own documentation requirements, and its own planning considerations. Missing a category means missing assets that may need to be included in the trust, updated with beneficiary designations, or located by whoever settles the estate.

1. Real Estate

Every property matters, regardless of where it is or how it's titled

Real estate is almost always the largest single asset in a parent's estate, and it's the one with the most planning implications. How a property is titled — solely in your parent's name, jointly with a spouse, in a trust, in an LLC — determines how it transfers at death and whether it goes through probate.

For each property, you need to know the address and current estimated value, how the title is held and in whose name, whether there is a mortgage and who holds it, whether the property is in the trust (and if not, why not), whether there is a life estate or any other legal interest affecting ownership, and the location of the deed.

If your parent owns property in more than one state, that multi-state ownership is a significant planning consideration. Each state where real property is titled may require its own probate proceeding unless the property is held in a trust. This is one of the clearest cases where a living trust saves meaningful time and money.

> ***Watch for this:*** *A property your parent thinks of as "in the trust" may not actually be titled in the trust's name. The deed is the controlling document, not the intention. Verify by pulling the deed, not by asking your parent.*

2. Bank and Credit Union Accounts

Checking, savings, CDs, and money market accounts

For each account, gather the institution name and branch, account numbers, approximate current balances, how the account is titled (solely, jointly, or in trust), and whether a payable-on-death (POD) beneficiary is designated.

A POD designation allows a bank account to transfer directly to the named beneficiary at death, bypassing probate similar in effect to having the account in a trust. If your parents' accounts have current, accurate POD designations, those accounts are handled. If the POD names a deceased person, an ex-spouse, or someone who should no longer be receiving those funds, it is a problem that needs fixing now.

Look also for accounts your parents may have forgotten about. A checking account from a bank they stopped using. A savings account opened for a grandchild that was never closed. A certificate of deposit that rolled over automatically for years. These things exist more often than families expect.

> **Practical step:** Ask your parents to pull three months of bank statements. Recurring deposits (Social Security, pension payments) and automatic bill payments tell you a lot about the full picture of their financial life without requiring them to remember every account.

3. Investment and Brokerage Accounts

Taxable accounts, mutual funds, stocks, and bonds

Investment accounts require the same information as bank accounts: institution, account numbers, approximate value, titling, and beneficiary designations. They also require attention to one additional consideration: cost basis.

Cost basis is what your parents originally paid for an investment. When they die, assets that pass to heirs receive what's called a stepped-up basis the cost basis resets to the fair market value at the date of death. This has significant tax implications for heirs who later sell those assets. An investment your parents bought for $20,000 that is now worth $150,000 would generate a $130,000 capital gain if sold during their lifetime. If it passes to a heir at death with a stepped-up basis of $150,000, and the heir sells it immediately, the taxable gain is zero.

This matters for planning. Assets with large, unrealized gains are often better candidates to pass through the estate rather than being gifted during life because gifting transfers the original cost basis along with the asset, while inheritance provides the step-up. Chapter 10 covers this in detail.

4. Retirement Accounts

IRAs, 401(k)s, 403(b)s, pensions, and annuities

Retirement accounts are governed by beneficiary designations, which override everything else including the will and the trust. This is one of the most important and most misunderstood facts in estate planning. It doesn't matter what your parents will say if the benefits on a retirement account names someone else. The designation wins.

For each retirement account, gather the institution and account type, approximate current value, and most critically the current primary and contingent beneficiary designations. Many people have never updated these designations since they first opened the account. A 401(k) opened at age 30 with a first spouse listed as beneficiary is a genuine problem if that person is deceased or divorced.

Also identify whether your parent has a pension a defined benefit plan from a former employer and if so, what the survivor benefit election was. If your parent elected a single-life pension (higher monthly payment but no benefit after death), that income stream ends when they die. If they elected a joint-and-survivor option, payments continue to a surviving spouse at a reduced amount. Both options affect estate planning calculations.

Retirement accounts generally should not be titled in a living trust doing so can trigger immediate taxation of the entire account. Instead, the trust can be named as the beneficiary, but this requires careful drafting to avoid tax complications. An elder law or estate planning attorney with retirement account experience should be involved in this decision. Chapter 10 addresses retirement account inheritance rules in full.

> **High priority:** Outdated beneficiary designations on retirement accounts are one of the most common and most costly estate planning failures. This is not paperwork that can wait. Pull the current designations and review them now.

5. Life Insurance Policies

Term, whole life, universal life, and group coverage

For each life insurance policy, gather the insurance company name and policy number, the death benefit amount, the policy owner (which matters for tax purposes), the current cash value if it's a permanent policy, the premium amount and payment schedule, and the primary and contingent beneficiary designations.

Like retirement accounts, life insurance passes by beneficiary designation and bypasses probate entirely — when the designations are current and accurate. When they're not, the problems are similar: benefits may flow to the wrong person, to a deceased person, or into the estate (where they do go through probate) if no living beneficiary is named.

Old group life insurance policies from past employers are commonly overlooked. Your parent may have worked somewhere for 20 years, left with a small pay-up policy, and completely forgotten about it. Contacting former employers or checking with state insurance regulators can sometimes surface policies that have been lost track of.

Also ask about any life insurance your parents own on someone else's life. This is less common but does occur, and the death benefit on such a policy would be an estate asset when your parent dies.

6. Digital Assets and Online Accounts

The category most families forget entirely

This is the newest and most overlooked category in estate planning, and it's growing more significant with every passing year.

Digital assets include financial accounts accessed only online (many people have investment or savings accounts they manage entirely through an app), cryptocurrency holdings, PayPal or Venmo balances, loyalty points and rewards with meaningful cash value, domain names, and online businesses or income streams.

They also include accounts with sentimental value that families often want to preserve or close email accounts, social media profiles, photo storage, and similar.

The practical problem with digital assets is access. Without usernames, passwords, and sometimes two-factor authentication codes, a deceased person's digital accounts are genuinely difficult to access and some platforms make account recovery by next of kin nearly impossible without legal documentation.

Your parent should document every significant digital account: the platform, the username or email associated with it, and the password. This document needs to be stored securely not in a text file on an unsecured computer and its location needs to be known to the successor trustee or executor. A password manager with a master password stored with the estate documents is one practical solution. A sealed envelope held by the attorney is another.

> ***Worth including:*** *Ask your parent about any automatic payments or subscriptions they manage online — streaming services, utilities, insurance premiums, charitable giving. These recurring transactions need to be identified and managed during any period of incapacity or estate settlement.*

7. Business Interests

Ownership stakes that require specific planning

If your parent owns a business, whether it's a sole proprietorship, a partnership interest, shares in a closely held corporation, or membership in an LLC, that interest is an estate asset that requires specific planning attention.

Business interests are often the most complex assets to handle in an estate. Their value may not be obvious. Their transfer may be governed by a buy-sell agreement that restricts who can inherit or acquire the interest. The business may have debts or obligations that affect the estate. And the business may depend on your parent's personal involvement in ways that affect its value at death.

If your parent has any business ownership, the inventory needs to capture the business name and structure, your parent's ownership percentage, the approximate value (or the basis for valuation), whether there is a buy-sell agreement and where it is located, and whether the business interest is held in the trust.

Business succession planning is a specialized area that goes beyond the scope of this book, but any estate plan involving a business interest needs to address it. An elder law or estate planning attorney with business succession experience should be part of the team.

8. Debts, Obligations, and Liabilities

What the estate owes, not just what it owns

A complete inventory isn't just assets. It's the full financial picture, which includes what your parents owe. Gather information on all outstanding mortgages (institution, balance, monthly payment, whether the property is in the trust), any home equity lines of credit, car loans, personal loans, credit card balances, and any co-signed debt that might affect the estate or surviving family members.

Also identify any ongoing financial obligations: alimony or support payments, guarantees on someone else's loan, outstanding pledges to charitable organizations, or any legal judgments. These obligations don't disappear at death they become claims against the estate.

Understanding the full picture of liabilities is essential for planning. An estate with $500,000 in assets and $200,000 in debts is very different from an estate with $500,000 in assets and

$20,000 in debts, and the planning strategy reflects that difference.

When Records Are Scattered, Incomplete, or Missing

Not every parent will hand you a neat folder with everything organized. Some parents have never been particularly organized. Others have been organized in ways that made sense to them but are opaque to everyone else. Some have lost documents in moves, floods, or fires. Some genuinely don't know what they have.

Here are the most reliable ways to reconstruct a financial picture when the records aren't readily available.

Tax returns

Your parents' last three to five years of federal tax returns are the single most useful document for identifying assets. Interest income reveals bank accounts. Dividend income reveals investment accounts. Schedule E reveals rental income and real estate. Schedule K-1 reveals business or partnership interests. Retirement distributions reveal account locations. If your parent uses a CPA or tax preparer, that person may be a valuable resource.

Mail and financial statements

A month of incoming mail — physical and electronic — is revealing. Financial institutions send annual statements, tax documents, and account notices. Insurance companies send premium notices. Government agencies send benefit statements. Going through recent mail with your parent's permission gives you a working list of institutions to contact.

Bank and credit card statements

Recurring automatic payments reveal ongoing obligations and accounts. Incoming deposits reveal income sources. Large or unusual transactions may reveal assets or transfers that need to be understood and accounted for.

State unclaimed property databases

Every state maintains a database of unclaimed property dormant bank accounts, uncashed checks, forgotten security deposits, and similar assets turned over to the state when institutions can't locate the owner. Searching your parents' name in their state's unclaimed property database (and in states where they previously lived) occasionally surfaces accounts they've genuinely forgotten about. The search is free and takes minutes.

Safe deposit boxes

If your parents have a safe deposit box, you need to know where it is and where the key is.

Safe deposit boxes routinely contain original documents deeds, birth certificates, marriage certificates, military records, insurance policies that are needed for estate settlement and may be difficult to replace. Many families discover a safe deposit box exists only during estate settlement, when accessing it requires a court order.

> **Action item:** Ask your parent directly: do you have a safe deposit box? If yes, where is it, where is the key, and who else has access? Write it down. Put it in the inventory.

The Quick-Reference Inventory Table

Use this table as a starting framework.

Asset / Document	Location / Institution	In the trust?
Primary residence		
Other real estate (vacation, rental)		
Checking account(s)		
Savings account(s)		
Certificates of deposit		
Investment / brokerage account(s)		
IRA(s)	N/A — use beneficiary designation	
401(k) / 403(b) / employer plan	N/A — use beneficiary designation	
Pension / defined benefit plan		

Life insurance policy(is)	N/A — use beneficiary designation	
Annuity(ies)		
Business ownership interest(s)		
Vehicles (cars, boats, RVs)		
Digital assets / online accounts		
Safe deposit box		
Outstanding debts / mortgages		

Keeping the Inventory Current

An inventory done once and never updated becomes a problem. Your parents' financial life changes: accounts open and close, property is bought and sold, beneficiary designations get updated (or should be). An inventory that reflects the situation from three years ago may miss assets acquired since then and include assets that no longer exist.

The inventory should be reviewed at the same time as the estate plan is reviewed — which Chapter 18 recommends at minimum every three years, and immediately after any significant life event: sale of a property, opening a new account, a new marriage, a significant gift, or any change in beneficiary designations.

Store the inventory somewhere the right people can find it. Not buried in a desk drawer. Not on a password-protected computer that nobody else can access. The successor trustee and executor need to be able to locate it, and they may be working under pressure and time constraints when they do. A copy with the estate attorney, a copy in a fireproof home safe with known access, and a copy with the successor trustee is a reasonable approach.

> ***Do not store it digitally without a backup:*** *A digital inventory on a single device that nobody else can access is nearly as bad as no inventory. Make sure at least one trusted person knows where the inventory is and can access it without your parent's assistance.*

The Inventory Is the Foundation

Everything that follows in this book — protecting the home, planning for long-term care, updating beneficiary designations, setting up the trust correctly — depends on knowing what's there. You cannot plan around assets you don't know exist. You cannot fund a trust with property you haven't identified. You cannot update a beneficiary designation you've forgotten about.

The inventory is not glamorous work. It's methodical and sometimes tedious, and it requires your parent's cooperation and patience. But it is the foundation that every other piece of the plan rests on, and doing it thoroughly now prevents an enormous amount of difficulty later.

Chapter 8 moves to the most significant single asset in most parents' estates: the family home. How to protect it, what happens to it if nursing home care becomes necessary, and what planning decisions need to be made now before those questions become urgent.

Each threat has solutions. None of the solutions are complicated. But they require deliberate action, and they require it before the crisis arrives.

CHAPTER 8

Protecting the Home and Major Assets

For most families, the home is the largest asset in the estate and the one with the most emotional weight. It is also the one most vulnerable to probate, nursing home costs, and planning mistakes. This chapter covers the strategies that protect it — and the ones that can backfire.

Why the Home Deserves Its Own Chapter

In a typical middle-class estate, the family home accounts for more than half the total value. It is often the only significant asset. It carries decades of memory, emotional meaning, and family history that no financial instrument can replicate. And it is frequently the asset that is worst protected — sitting in your parent's name alone, unprotected from probate, unprotected from the cost of long-term care, unprotected from the complications that arise in blended families or between siblings who don't agree.

Protecting the home requires understanding three distinct threats and addressing each one directly. The first is probate — the public, slow, expensive legal process that a solely owned home triggers at death. The second is the cost of nursing home care and Medicaid's reach into assets. The third is unintended outcomes that arise from how the home is titled, gifted, or transferred without proper planning.

Each threat has solutions. None of the solutions are complicated. But they require deliberate action, and they require it before the crisis arrives — not after.

How the Living Trust Protects Real Estate from Probate

The most straightforward protection for the family home is the one that Chapter 4 introduced: a properly funded revocable living trust. When a home is titled in the trust's name, it transfers to the named beneficiaries at death without any court involvement, on a timeline measured in weeks rather than months or years, at a fraction of the cost of probate.

The mechanics are simple. The attorney prepares a new deed transferring the property from your parent's individual name to the trust — typically "John Smith, as trustee of the John

Smith Revocable Living Trust dated January 1, 2024." That deed is recorded with the county recorder. From that point, the trust owns the home. Your parents continue to live in it, manage it, sell it, or make any changes they want because they are also the trustee, and the trust is revocable. Nothing about their day-to-day relationship with the property changes.

When they die, the successor trustee steps in and transfers the home to the beneficiaries according to the trust's terms. No probate. No court filing. No public record of the estate's value or the identities of the beneficiaries. No window for creditors to file claims through a public probate proceeding.

The transfer of real estate into a trust does not trigger a due-on-sale clause in a mortgage, does not affect homestead exemptions in most states, and does not affect property tax exemptions in most states. It does not constitute a gift for Medicaid purposes because the trust is revocable, your parent retains full control. An elder law attorney can confirm the specific rules in your parent's state.

> ***The key step:*** *Signing the trust document is not enough. The deed must be drawn up, signed, and recorded with the county to move the property into the trust. This is the funding step that many families miss. Verify it was done by pulling the current deed from the county recorder's office — most counties make this searchable online for free.*

Other Ways to Transfer a Home Outside of Probate

A revocable living trust is the most comprehensive and flexible solution for most families. But it is not the only way to keep the home out of probate, and understanding the alternatives helps you evaluate what is right for your parent's specific situation.

Joint Tenancy with Right of Survivorship

Simple but limited — and not without risks

Joint tenancy with right of survivorship (JTWROS) means that two or more people own the property together, and when one dies, their share automatically passes to the surviving owner without probate. For a married couple who own their home jointly, this works cleanly during their lifetimes — when one spouse dies, the other becomes the sole owner automatically.

The problem is what happens next. When the surviving spouse dies, the home is now solely in their name, and without a trust or other planning, it goes through probate. Joint tenancy solves the first death problem; it does not solve the second.

Adding an adult child as a joint tenant to solve this problem creates its own issues. The child immediately owns a partial interest in the property, which means their creditors, divorcing spouses, or legal judgments can potentially reach that interest. It also means the child's consent is now required to sell the home something that can complicate decisions if the parent's situation changes. And it creates a gift tax consideration if the value of the interest transferred exceeds the annual gift exclusion.

Joint tenancy is a useful tool in specific circumstances. It is not a substitute for a living trust when real estate is involved.

Life Estate Deed

Keeps the home out of probate and preserves some Medicaid protection — with trade-offs

A life estate deed is a legal arrangement in which your parent transfer ownership of the home to their children (or other beneficiaries) while retaining the right to live in and control the property for the rest of their life. At death, the property passes automatically to the remainder beneficiaries the children without probate.

The Medicaid angle is where this gets interesting. Because your parents have transferred the home, it may not be counted as a countable asset for Medicaid eligibility purposes after the five-year lookback period has passed. A life estate deed created more than five years before a Medicaid application is generally not subject to Medicaid recovery in most states. This makes it a useful planning tool for families worried about nursing home costs eating through the home's value.

The trade-offs are real, though. Once a life estate deed is recorded, your parents cannot sell the home, refinance it, or change the beneficiaries without the consent of the remainder beneficiaries the children. They give up full control, even though they retain the right to live there. If family dynamics change a child goes through a divorce, develops financial problems, or has a falling out with the parent unwinding a life estate is complicated and sometimes impossible without litigation.

A life estate deed also does not provide the same flexibility as a trust. It cannot include detailed instructions about how the property should be managed, cannot easily accommodate changes in beneficiaries, and cannot be updated without executing a new deed.

Transfer on Death Deed

The simplest option — available in about half of states

A transfer on death (TOD) deed — also called a beneficiary deed or Lady Bird deed in some states — allows your parent to name a beneficiary who receives the property automatically at death, while your parent retains complete control and ownership during their lifetime. Unlike a life estate, the beneficiary has no current ownership interest and no rights until your parent dies. Your parent can sell, mortgage, change the beneficiary, or revoke the deed entirely at any time.

Where it is available, the TOD deed is arguably the simplest way to keep a home out of probate for families who don't need the broader protection of a living trust. It accomplishes the core probate-avoidance goal without the cost and complexity of a full trust setup.

The limitation is availability. As of this writing, TOD deeds are recognized in approximately half of U.S. states. They are not available everywhere, and even where they are available, they are subject to state-specific rules about execution, recording, and revocation. An elder law attorney in your parent's state can confirm whether this option exists and whether it makes sense for their situation.

> ***Check availability first:*** *Do not assume a TOD deed is available in your parent's state. Search the state's real property laws or ask an attorney. Using an instrument that isn't legally recognized produces results that may not hold up.*

What Happens to the Home If a Parent Needs Nursing Home Care

This is the question that genuinely frightens families, and it deserves a direct answer.

Nursing home care in the United States is extraordinarily expensive — costs, timelines, and coverage details are addressed in depth in Chapter 9 but the short version is that a year in a skilled nursing facility typically costs between $80,000 and $120,000 or more depending on location. Medicare covers a limited rehabilitation period. After that, families pay out of pocket until they qualify for Medicaid.

Medicaid is the government program that covers long-term nursing home care for people who meet the financial eligibility requirements. To qualify, your parents must have very limited assets. In most states, the asset limit is around $2,000 in countable assets for a single person. The home, however, is generally exempt if the Medicaid recipient intends to return there, or if a qualifying spouse or dependent person lives there.

The problem comes at death or when the parent moves permanently to a nursing home and the home is no longer their primary residence. At that point, many states have Medicaid estate recovery programs that allow the state to seek reimbursement for Medicaid benefits paid during the person's lifetime from the assets of their estate, including the home.

This means a family that assumed the home would pass to the children can instead find that the state has a claim against it sometimes for hundreds of thousands of dollars in Medicaid benefits — before anything passes to heirs.

> *Medicaid doesn't take the house while your parent is alive. It comes for the estate afterward. That distinction is what catches families off guard.*

The Five-Year Lookback Rule: What It Is and Why It Matters

Medicaid has a five-year lookback rule that examines every asset transfer your parent made in the five years before applying for Medicaid long-term care benefits. If your parent transferred the home — or any other significant asset — to their children during that five-year window, Medicaid treats it as an improper transfer and imposes a penalty period during which your parent is ineligible for benefits.

The penalty period is calculated by dividing the value of the transferred assets by the average monthly cost of nursing home care in your parent's state. Transfer a $250,000 home in a state where nursing home care averages $8,000 per month, and the penalty period is approximately 31 months during which Medicaid will not pay for care a period during which your parent is expected to pay out of pocket from assets they no longer have.

This is why timing is so critical. Medicaid planning that involves asset transfers needs to happen at least five years before a Medicaid application is likely to be filed. For a parent in their mid-60s who is healthy, that window is open. For a parent who is already showing signs of cognitive decline or who has just received a serious diagnosis, the window may be closing or already closed.

The lookback rule applies to transfers made for less than fair market value. A gift. A sale at a reduced price. A transfer to a trust that the parent no longer controls. A life estate deed. Any of these, if made within the five-year window, can trigger a penalty period.

> ***The planning principle:*** *If Medicaid protection for the home is a goal, the planning*

needs to start now — not when nursing home care appears imminent. Five years is not a long time when a health situation can change without warning.

Medicaid Asset Protection Trusts and the Home

A Medicaid Asset Protection Trust (MAPT) is an irrevocable trust specifically designed to hold assets including the home in a way that protects them from Medicaid recovery after the five-year lookback period has passed. Once the home is transferred into a MAPT and five years have elapsed, it is generally protected from the state's Medicaid estate recovery claim.

The critical distinction between a MAPT and a revocable living trust: the MAPT is irrevocable. Your parents give up control of the asset. They cannot take the home back out of the trust, cannot change the beneficiaries, and cannot sell the home and keep the proceeds without the trustee's involvement. In exchange for that loss of control, the asset gains Medicaid protection after the lookback period.

Your parents can typically retain the right to live in the home and receive any income generated by it. The home itself, the principal, is protected. If the home is sold, however, the proceeds generally stay in the trust rather than being distributed to your parent directly, because distributing them to your parent would make them a countable asset again.

MAPTs are legitimate, widely used, and legally sound when done correctly. They are also complex. The drafting needs to be done by an elder law attorney with specific Medicaid planning experience. The rules vary by state. And the timing — the five-year clock starting from when assets are transferred into the trust — needs to be carefully considered in the context of your parent's current health and likely timeline.

> ***Not a DIY project:*** *A Medicaid Asset Protection Trust done incorrectly can disqualify your parent from Medicaid rather than protecting them, expose assets to recovery that should have been protected, and create tax problems that outweigh the benefits. This is one area where experienced legal counsel is non-negotiable.*

The Outright Gift Problem

One of the most common instincts families have when they start worrying about nursing home costs is to simply give the home to the children. Transfer it now, get it out of your parent's name, and protect it from Medicaid recovery.

This approach has three significant problems that make it a poor choice in most situations.

The first is the five-year lookback. An outright gift of the home to a child is exactly the kind of transfer Medicaid examines, and if the gift was made within five years of a Medicaid application, it triggers a penalty period. The gift doesn't protect the asset it just creates a timing problem.

The second is the loss of the stepped-up basis. When your parents give the home to a child, that child receives the home on your parent's original cost basis. If your parents bought the home in 1978 for $80,000 and it is now worth $380,000, the child who receives it as a gift has a cost basis of $80,000. If they later sell it, they owe capital gains tax on $300,000 of gain. If they had inherited it instead, the cost basis would reset to $380,000 at the date of your parent's death, a stepped-up basis and the sale would generate no capital gain at all. Gifting the home during life can cost the family tens of thousands of dollars in taxes compared to simply leaving it in the estate.

The third is the loss of control. Once the home is in a child's name, the child owns it. Their creditors, their divorcing spouse, their legal judgments can reach it. If the child predeceases the parent, the home becomes part of the child's estate. If the family relationship deteriorates, the parent has no legal recourse — they gave away their home.

Outright gifting of the family home is rarely the right strategy. The combination of Medicaid lookback exposure, lost basis step-up, and complete loss of control makes it a poor trade-off in almost every situation where better alternatives exist.

Comparing the Options: A Decision Framework

The right strategy for protecting the family home depends on your parent's specific situation: their age and health, the home's value and how long they've owned it, whether nursing home care is a near-term or distant concern, and the family dynamics involved. The table below provides a framework for comparing the most common approaches.

Transfer Method	Avoids Probate?	Protects from Medicaid?	Retains Step-Up in Basis?
Revocable living trust	Yes	No	Yes
Joint tenancy (JTWROS)	Yes	No	Partial (50%)
Life estate deed	Yes	Partial (after 5-	Yes

		year lookback)	
Transfer on Death (TOD) deed	Yes (where available)	No	Yes
Irrevocable trust (MAPT)	Yes	Yes (after 5-year lookback)	Yes
Outright gift to children	Yes	Yes (after 5-year lookback)	No — loses step-up
No plan — solely owned	No — goes through probate	No	Yes

The right choice for most families with no immediate nursing home concern and a primary goal of avoiding probate is a revocable living trust. For families with a more immediate concern about Medicaid exposure and enough time to clear the five-year lookback, a MAPT deserves serious consideration. For families in states where it's available and who want a simpler solution, a TOD deed may be adequate. A life estate deed occupies a middle ground that suits some situations well.

No single strategy is right for everyone. An elder law attorney who understands both the state-specific rules and your parent's complete financial picture is the right person to help navigate this decision.

Protecting Other Major Assets

The home gets most of the attention, but it is not the only major asset that deserves deliberate planning. Investment accounts, business interests, and other significant assets each have their own vulnerabilities and their own protective strategies.

Investment and brokerage accounts

Taxable investment accounts held solely in your parent's name go through probate at death unless they are held in a trust or have a transfer on death (TOD) beneficiary designation. Most brokerage firms allow account holders to designate a TOD beneficiary, which transfers the account directly at death without probate. If your parent's brokerage accounts don't have current, accurate TOD designations, adding them is a simple and free update that significantly simplifies estate settlement.

If the accounts are large enough to warrant it, holding them in the living trust rather than relying solely on TOD designations provides additional flexibility particularly if your parent becomes incapacitated, because the trustee can manage trust assets without needing separate authority.

Vehicles

Cars, boats, and other titled vehicles generally cannot be held in a living trust in most states, and the administrative cost of trying to do so usually exceeds the benefit. Most states allow transfer on death designations for vehicle titles, which is the simplest solution. Alternatively, vehicles are often handled through a simplified probate procedure for small estates, particularly if the vehicle's value is modest. Check your parents' state's specific rules.

Business interests

A business interest held in a living trust transfers without probate at death. Whether that's the right approach depends heavily on the business structure, any existing buy- sell agreements, and the succession plan for the business itself. This is one of the more complex planning situations, and it requires coordination between the estate plan and the business succession plan. Chapter 7 flagged this, and it bears repeating: any estate involving a business ownership interest needs an attorney with business succession experience involved in the planning.

Retirement accounts and life insurance

As noted in Chapter 7, these assets pass by beneficiary designation and should not be held in a revocable living trust directly. The protection strategy for retirement accounts and life insurance is current, accurate, and thoughtfully chosen beneficiary designations not trust titling. Chapter 10 covers beneficiary designation strategy in full.

Protection Requires Deliberate Action

The family home does not protect itself. A lifetime of mortgage payments and careful ownership does not automatically ensure that the asset ends up where your parents intend, at the lowest possible cost, with the lowest possible disruption to the family.

That outcome requires a deed drawn up and recorded. A trust properly funded. A strategy for nursing home costs that starts far enough in advance to be effective. Deliberate choices about titling and transfer mechanisms that reflect your parent's actual situation and goals.

None of this is complicated once you understand the options. But it requires action, and that action needs to happen before the crisis — not as a response to it.

Chapter 9 moves deeper into the long-term care question: what nursing home and in- home care cost, what Medicare and Medicaid cover, and how families can plan for costs that have a way of destroying unprepared estates.

CHAPTER 9

Long-Term Care: The Cost That Destroys Unprepared Families

Long-term care is the single largest unplanned financial risk most aging families face. Medicare covers almost none of it. The cost of doing nothing is catastrophic. This chapter breaks down what care costs, what coverage exists, and what planning works.

The Assumption That Destroys Estates

Most families carry a quiet assumption that Medicare will handle nursing home costs if it ever comes to that. It is one of the most widespread and most costly misconceptions in personal finance.

Medicare is health insurance. It covers hospitalizations, physician visits, prescription drugs, and medically necessary treatments. What it does not cover with very limited exceptions is the cost of custodial care. The daily assistance with bathing, dressing, eating, and moving that defines long-term care. The kind of care that becomes necessary not because of a specific acute medical condition but because of the slow accumulation of frailty, cognitive decline, or chronic illness.

That distinction between medical care and custodial care is the gap that catches families completely unprepared. Your parent can be a Medicare beneficiary in perfect standing, with supplemental coverage on top, and still face nursing home costs of $9,000 to $14,000 per month that Medicare will not touch after the first 20 days of a qualifying skilled care stay.

A two-year stay in a skilled nursing facility at median national rates costs somewhere between $180,000 and $280,000. A three-year stay crosses $300,000. These are not outlier numbers. The average length of long-term care for someone over 65 who needs it is approximately three years. Roughly one in five people will need it for more than five years.

An estate that looks solid on paper a paid-off home, $200,000 in savings, a modest investment account — can be entirely consumed by long-term care costs before Medicaid eligibility kicks in. That is not a planning failure. It is what happens when no planning occurs at all.

> *Long-term care doesn't just affect your parent's finances. It affects yours. Families that haven't planned for this cost often end up making impossible choices between their own financial stability and their parent's care needs.*

What Long-Term Care Actually Costs

The numbers below represent national averages and ranges. Costs vary significantly by geography — care in rural areas of the Midwest costs considerably less than care in metropolitan coastal areas — and they increase year over year. Use these figures as a framework, then research current rates in your parent's specific area.

Type of Care	Monthly Cost (Low)	Monthly Cost (High)	Medicare Covers?
In-home aide (part-time, 20 hrs/wk)	$1,800	$3,600	No
In-home aide (full-time, 44 hrs/wk)	$4,500	$7,500	No
Adult day care program	$1,200	$2,800	No
Assisted living facility	$3,500	$7,000	No
Memory care facility	$5,000	$9,000	No
Skilled nursing facility (semi-private)	$7,500	$11,000	Days 1–20 only (after qualifying stay)
Skilled nursing facility (private room)	$9,000	$14,000+	Days 1–20 only (after qualifying stay)

A few things stand out in those numbers. In-home care, which most families assume is the inexpensive option, is not inexpensive once the hours add up. Full-time in-home care for a parent who cannot be left alone costs as much or more than assisted living in many markets. Assisted living is not covered by Medicare and is covered by Medicaid only sporadically depending on the state. And skilled nursing facility costs, even at the low end, represent a financial commitment that most families cannot sustain from savings alone beyond 18 to 24 months.

The question is not whether your parent might need this care. Statistics say roughly 70 percent of people over 65 will need some form of long-term care. The question is how the cost will be funded.

> ***Local research:*** *The Genworth Cost of Care Survey publishes annual long-term care cost data broken down by state and city. It is free, updated annually, and is the most reliable source for understanding what care costs in your parent's specific market.*

Medicare vs. Medicaid: What Each One Actually Covers

The confusion between Medicare and Medicaid is so pervasive that it is worth addressing directly and in detail. These are two entirely different programs with different eligibility rules, different coverage, and different implications for estate planning.

	Medicare	Medicaid
What it is	Federal health insurance for people 65+	Federal/state program for low-income individuals
Who qualifies	Anyone 65+ (or with qualifying disability)	People who meet income and asset limits
Covers skilled nursing care?	Days 1–20 at 100%; Days 21–100 with co-pay; nothing after Day 100	Yes — indefinitely, once eligible
Covers custodial / personal care?	No	Yes — in qualifying facilities and some home settings
Covers assisted living?	No	Sometimes — varies significantly by state

Asset limits to qualify	None	Approximately $2,000 (single); varies by state
Estate recovery after death?	No	Yes — in most states, for benefits paid after 55

The key takeaway from that table: Medicare is short-term medical coverage. After 100 days in a skilled nursing facility and only if the stay followed a qualifying hospital admission of at least three days — Medicare stops paying entirely. From Day 101 forward, your parents pay out of pocket until they have spent down enough assets to qualify for Medicaid.

Medicaid is the program that funds long-term nursing home care for most Americans who can't afford to pay privately. But qualifying for Medicaid requires meeting strict asset and income limits and qualifying while protecting what your parents has built requires advance planning often years in advance.

> ***The Medicare SNF trap:*** *Many families are blindsided when Medicare's nursing home coverage ends. The transition from Medicare-covered care to private pay to Medicaid can happen faster than families anticipate, and each transition point requires decisions about care level, facility, and finances that are much harder to make well without prior planning.*

Long-Term Care Insurance: What It Covers and When It's Too Late

Long-term care insurance is a policy that pays a daily or monthly benefit toward qualifying care costs in-home care, assisted living, memory care, or skilled nursing when the insured person can no longer perform a specified number of activities of daily living (typically two of six: bathing, dressing, eating, continence, transferring, and toileting) or has a cognitive impairment.

For families who purchased a policy 10 or 20 years ago, it may be the most asset in the estate plan. A good long-term care policy can cover $150 to $300 per day in benefits for two to five years or longer, with an inflation rider that increases the benefit over time. That coverage can mean the difference between choosing any facility and choosing whatever Medicaid approves.

The problem is that long-term care insurance has become significantly more expensive and harder to obtain than it was in previous decades. Insurers dramatically underestimated claim costs in their original pricing, which led to major premium increases, benefit reductions, and several large carriers existing in the market entirely.

Today, a comprehensive long-term care policy for couples in their mid-60s can cost $4,000 to $8,000 or more per year in premiums, and the premiums are not fixed they can increase with state regulatory approval.

When it makes sense

Long-term care insurance is most worth considering for parents in their late 50s to mid- 60s who are in good health, can afford the premiums without straining their budget, and have assets worth protecting that are above the Medicaid threshold but below the level where they could comfortably self-fund several years of care.

At roughly $200,000 to $2,000,000 in liquid assets, long-term care insurance plays a meaningful protective role. Below $200,000, the spend-down to Medicaid eligibility may happen regardless. Above $2,000,000, many families have enough to self-fund care without meaningfully depleting the estate.

When it is too late

Long-term care insurance requires medical underwriting. A parent who has already been diagnosed with Alzheimer's, Parkinson's, a recent stroke, or several other conditions will not qualify. A parent who is already showing significant cognitive decline will not qualify. The window for obtaining coverage closes before most families think to open it.

If your parents are in their early to mid-60s and healthy, have the conversation about long-term care insurance now. If they are in their mid-70s with any significant health history, the window may be closed and other strategies Medicaid planning, asset protection trusts, self-funding strategies — need to take priority.

Hybrid and linked-benefit policies

In response to the traditional long-term care insurance market's instability, a new category of hybrid policies has emerged that links long-term care benefits to a life insurance policy or annuity. If care is needed, the policy pays benefits toward care costs. If care is never needed, the policy pays a death benefit. The premiums are typically fixed and paid as a lump sum or over a defined period rather than ongoing annual premiums.

Hybrid policies trade some of the benefit richness of traditional long-term care policies for premium stability and the elimination of the "use it or lose it" concern. They are worth exploring for families where traditional coverage is not available or affordable, but the specifics vary enormously by product and should be evaluated with an independent financial advisor.

Medicaid Planning: The Strategy and the Limits

For families whose parents cannot obtain long-term care insurance, cannot afford to self- fund extended care, and have meaningful assets worth protecting, Medicaid planning is the primary strategy. Chapter 8 introduced the five-year lookback rule and Medicaid Asset Protection Trusts in the context of the family home. This section covers the broader Medicaid planning picture.

What Medicaid counts and what it doesn't

Medicaid distinguishes between countable assets — which must be spent down to meet eligibility limits and exempt assets, which are not counted. The rules are complex and vary by state, but the broad framework is consistent.

Countable assets generally include bank accounts and investment accounts, retirement accounts (in most states), second homes and vacation properties, and vehicles beyond one primary vehicle. The combined countable asset limit for a single Medicaid applicant is approximately $2,000 in most states.

Exempt assets generally include the primary residence (subject to estate recovery), one vehicle, personal property and household goods, a small amount of burial funds, and certain other protected assets. A spouse who remains living at home — called the community spouse — is entitled to a protected amount of the couple's assets called the Community Spouse Resource Allowance (CSRA), which varies by state but currently ranges from approximately $30,000 to $148,000.

The spend-down reality

For families without advance planning, the path to Medicaid eligibility is spend-down: paying for care out of pocket until countable assets reach the eligibility limit, at which point Medicaid takes over. On a $150,000 liquid savings balance with nursing home costs of $9,000 per month, spend-down takes roughly 16 months. On a $300,000 savings balance, approximately 33 months. The home is protected during this period if the parent intends to return or a spouse life there, but it becomes subject to estate recovery after death.

Spend-down is not a failure of planning it is simply the absence of planning. It is the default path. Medicaid planning is the deliberate alternative.

Permissible Medicaid planning strategies

Not all asset transfers are improper under Medicaid rules. Several strategies are explicitly permitted and can significantly reduce the assets subject to spend down while staying within legal boundaries.

Paying off debts is always permissible a parent approaching Medicaid eligibility can pay off a mortgage, car loan, or other debt without triggering a penalty. Home improvements are permissible. Prepaying funeral and burial expenses up to state- allowed limits is permissible. Converting countable assets to exempt assets for example, purchasing a pre-paid burial contract or a single-premium immediate annuity structured to comply with Medicaid rules can be permissible depending on the state.

Community spouse protections allow significant asset preservation for married couples. A spouse who remains at home is entitled to keep the CSRA plus the home plus a protected monthly income allowance. Married couples facing nursing home costs have more tools available than single individuals.

Medicaid Asset Protection Trusts, as covered in Chapter 8, protect assets placed in them after the five-year lookback period has elapsed. For families with the time to implement them, they are the most comprehensive protection available.

> **Know your state's rules:** Medicaid rules vary dramatically by state. Eligibility thresholds, exempt asset categories, estate recovery policies, and permissible planning strategies differ in ways that make state-specific legal advice non- negotiable. A strategy that works in one state may be penalized in another. Always work with an elder law attorney licensed in your parent's state.

Planning for In-Home Care, Assisted Living, and Skilled Nursing

Long-term care is not a single thing. It is a spectrum that most families move along gradually, and the planning considerations at each stage are different.

In-home care

Most people prefer to remain at home as long as possible, and with appropriate support, many can. In-home care ranges from a few hours of assistance per week to full-time live-in care, and the cost scales accordingly. The critical planning question for in-home care is who pays for it.

Medicare covers short-term skilled nursing visits at home following a hospitalization, but not ongoing personal care. Medicaid covers some in-home care in most states through home and community-based services (HCBS) waiver programs, but these programs frequently have waiting lists. Long-term care insurance with an in-home benefit covers a daily or monthly amount toward hired care. Out-of-pocket funding is the default for families without other coverage.

For families where an adult child provides substantial in-home care, a formal caregiver agreement a written contract that pays the caregiver a market rate for their services can accomplish two things simultaneously: it fairly compensates the caregiver for genuine work, and it transfers assets from the parent to the caregiver in a way that Medicaid generally treats as compensation rather than a gift, avoiding the lookback penalty. The agreement must be in writing, must pay at market rates, and should be established before Medicaid planning becomes urgent.

Assisted living

Assisted living facilities provide housing, meals, medication management, and personal care assistance in a residential setting for people who need support but not the intensive medical care of a skilled nursing facility. They are not covered by Medicare.

Medicaid covers assisted living in some states through waiver programs, but coverage is inconsistent and the quality and availability of Medicaid-approved facilities varies widely.

For most families, assisted living is a private-pay proposition. Monthly costs range from $3,500 to $7,000 at the national median, with memory care units running significantly higher. Long-term care insurance that includes an assisted living benefit and most modern policies do can offset a meaningful portion of this cost.

The transition from home to assisted living is often the first significant financial planning inflection point. It is the moment when families realize that care costs are no longer theoretical they are showing up in bank statements every month.

Skilled nursing facility

A skilled nursing facility (SNF) provides 24-hour medical supervision and nursing care for people who require a level of medical attention that cannot be safely provided at home or in assisted living. The cost is the highest of any long-term care setting, and the path to Medicaid coverage once private assets are spent down runs directly through this setting.

Choosing a skilled nursing facility is a consequential decision. Medicaid covers nursing home care at approved facilities, but the quality of Medicaid-approved facilities varies significantly.

Families who plan ahead, who have protected assets, maintained long term care insurance, or have resources available from Medicaid planning — have more choices. Families who arrive at the nursing home door in spend-down crisis go where Medicaid will pay, which may not be where they would have chosen.

Medicare's nursing home website (medicare.gov/care-compare) provides five-star quality ratings for every certified nursing facility in the country. Researching facilities before they're needed identifying which ones in your parent's area have strong quality ratings and accept Medicaid is a worthwhile exercise that most families only think to do under pressure.

Having a Long-Term Care Conversation with Your Parent

This is a harder conversation than the estate planning conversation for most families, because it requires your parents to confront not just mortality but the loss of independence and physical capacity that they fear most.

Frame it around choices and preferences rather than problems and costs. What would your parents want if they needed help? Where would they want to live? Who would they want involved in their care? What matters most to them about their quality of life? These questions invite your parents to articulate preferences that then drive the planning decisions rather than confronting them with a financial crisis they haven't thought about.

Get specific about their existing coverage. Do they have a long-term care policy? Do they know what it covers? Where is it? Have they looked at it recently? A surprising number of families discover that an existing policy has more or less coverage than anyone remembered, or that premiums have lapsed and coverage is no longer in force.

And address the family capacity question directly. Who would be available to provide care, and at what cost to their own lives and careers? The assumption that a family member will step in — usually a daughter or daughter-in-law, statistically speaking without compensation or support is a plan. It is just usually not a fair or sustainable one. Naming it and planning around it explicitly is better than leaving it unspoken.

> ***Useful exercise:*** *Ask your parents to describe their ideal situation if they could no longer manage at home safely. Where would they want to be? Who would they want to help them? What would they not want to happen? Their answers are the foundation of the care plan.*

The Intersection with the Estate Plan

Long-term care planning and estate planning are not separate topics. They interact in ways that make coordinating them essential. The assets protected through Medicaid planning a home in a MAPT, assets transferred more than five years before a Medicaid application are still part of the estate plan. The trust that holds the home for Medicaid protection also needs to address how the home transfers to heirs at death. The long-term care insurance benefit that pays for care is an asset that needs to be identified in the inventory and understood by the successor trustee. The caregiver agreement that compensates an adult child for care affects both the estate's asset base and the sibling equity question that Chapter 3 covered.

This is why the same attorney specifically; an elder law attorney rather than a general estate planning attorney should ideally handle both the estate plan and any Medicaid planning. Elder law attorneys specialize in exactly this intersection. They understand how long-term care costs interact with estate planning decisions, how Medicaid rules apply in their specific state, and how to structure documents that address both goals simultaneously.

A general estate planning attorney can draft a perfectly good will and trust. An elder law attorney can do that and help your family navigate the Medicaid rules, evaluate long-term care insurance options, set up a MAPT if appropriate, and coordinate the full picture. For families where long-term care costs are a meaningful concern which is most families the elder law specialty is worth seeking out specifically.

The Cost of Doing Nothing

Long-term care planning is the area where the cost of inaction is most quantifiable and most devastating. A family that has protected the home through a trust or MAPT, maintained a long-term care insurance policy, and understood the Medicaid rules in advance has options when care becomes necessary. They can choose the facility. They can maintain quality. They can protect what their parent built.

A family that did none of that spends down every asset over 18 to 36 months, then goes wherever Medicaid will pay, with no negotiating position and no protected inheritance to pass on.

Both paths start from the same place: an aging parent with a home, some savings, and no immediate crisis. The difference between them is entirely in what the family chose to do while there was still time to do it.

Chapter 10 moves to the tax and beneficiary decisions that quietly cost heirs thousands of dollars outdated designations, capital gains traps, retirement account inheritance rules, and the mistakes most families don't find out about until it's too late to fix them.

CHAPTER 10

Taxes, Beneficiaries, and the Mistakes That Cost Heirs Thousands

---

The most expensive estate planning mistakes are often the quietest ones. An outdated beneficiary designation. A misunderstood tax rule. A retirement account inherited the wrong way. This chapter covers the decisions that look like paperwork details but carry five-figure consequences.

Why Beneficiary Designations Override Everything

Here is a rule that most families do not fully absorb until it costs them: a beneficiary designation on a financial account overrides the will. It overrides the trust. It overrides any verbal promise your parent ever made. It overrides any written instruction that is not the designation form itself.

When your parent named a beneficiary on a retirement account, a life insurance policy, a bank account with a payable-on-death designation, or a brokerage account with a transfer-on-death designation, that naming is a legally binding contract with the financial institution. At death, the institution distributes the asset to whoever is named on that form — without consulting the will, without asking the family, and without any court involvement.

This is powerful when the designations are current and accurate. It is catastrophic when they are not.

A parent who remarried fifteen years ago and never updated the beneficiary designations on their 401(k) may have their first spouse still named as primary beneficiary. A parent who named their own parent as beneficiary decades ago may have a deceased person named. A parent who had a falling out with one child and changed their will but forgot to update the IRA designation may inadvertently leave that child the largest single asset in the estate.

None of these outcomes require bad intent. They require nothing more than paperwork that was never updated. And unlike a mistake in a will, which can sometimes be corrected before it takes effect, a beneficiary designation error is typically discovered only after the death — at which point it is too late to fix.

> *The will governs what the will covers. Everything else is governed by the designation on file. If those two documents point in different directions, the designation wins.*

The Most Common Beneficiary Designation Mistakes

Beneficiary designation errors fall into recognizable patterns. The table below covers the most common ones, what they produce, and how to fix them before they cause damage.

The Mistake	What Happens	How to Fix It
Deceased spouse or parent named as primary	Account passes to contingent beneficiary or falls into estate and goes through probate	Update designation immediately to living beneficiaries
Ex-spouse still named after divorce	Ex-spouse receives the asset — in most states, courts cannot override a beneficiary designation	Update all designations immediately upon divorce
No contingent beneficiary named	If primary predeceases, asset falls into estate and goes through probate	Always name at least one contingent beneficiary
Minor child named as direct beneficiary	Court appoints a guardian to manage funds until the child turns 18, then gives the child full control at 18	Name a trust as beneficiary with distribution terms for minors

Estate named as beneficiary	Asset goes through probate, loses tax deferral advantages, and creditors can reach it	Name a living person or properly drafted trust instead
Trust named without proper qualifying language	Retirement account loses stretch provisions, entire account may become taxable within 5 years	Work with attorney to ensure trust meets IRS requirements as a designated beneficiary

The ex-spouse scenario deserves particular emphasis. In some states, divorce automatically revokes a beneficiary designation to a former spouse on certain accounts. In many states, it does not — and even in states where it does, that protection may not extend to all account types. A parent who divorces and does not actively update every beneficiary designation is gambling on state law, and that is a gamble that families have lost in court repeatedly. Update designations immediately upon any divorce, and review them again at remarriage.

The minor child scenario is equally important and more commonly overlooked. Naming a minor child as a direct beneficiary of a life insurance policy or retirement account means a court will appoint a guardian of the property to manage those funds until the child reaches adulthood — at which point the child receives the full amount with no restrictions. A 18-year-old who inherits $200,000 outright has no obligation to use it wisely. A trust as beneficiary, with thoughtfully written distribution terms, puts guardrails on the timing and purpose of distributions.

> ***Action item:*** *Pull every beneficiary designation your parent has on file across all accounts — retirement accounts, life insurance, bank accounts with POD designations, brokerage accounts with TOD designations. Review them against who your parent actually wants to receive those assets. Update anything that is incorrect, outdated, or missing a contingent beneficiary.*

Capital Gains and the Stepped-Up Basis

Chapter 8 introduced the stepped-up basis in the context of gifting the family home. The same principle applies to every appreciated asset in your parent's estate, and understanding it changes how thoughtful families approach lifetime gifting decisions.

When someone dies, assets that pass to heirs receive a new cost basis equal to the fair market value at the date of death. This reset the stepped-up basis means that any appreciation that occurred during your parent's lifetime is never taxed as capital gains. It disappears at death.

When someone gives an asset away during their lifetime, the recipient takes the donor's original cost basis. The appreciation that occurred during the donor's lifetime is preserved inside the asset, and the recipient will eventually owe capital gains tax on all of it when they sell.

	Gifted During Life	Inherited at Death
Original purchase price (your parent's basis)	$40,000	$40,000
Fair market value at transfer	$280,000	$280,000
Heir's cost basis	$40,000 (carries over)	$280,000 (stepped up)
Heir sells for $280,000	Taxable gain: $240,000	Taxable gain: $0
Capital gains tax owed (at 15%)	$36,000	$0

That $36,000 difference in the table above is real money that leaves the family unnecessarily. And the example uses a modest appreciation scenario. A stock your parent bought in 1990 for $10,000 that is now worth $180,000 represents $170,000 in unrealized gain. Gifted during life, the heir ultimately owes capital gains tax on $170,000. Inherited at death, the heir owes nothing.

The planning implication is direct: assets with large unrealized gains are generally better candidates for inheritance than for lifetime gifting. Assets with little or no appreciation — or assets that have declined in value — are better candidates for lifetime gifting if gifting is part of the plan.

This does not mean your parent should never give appreciated assets during their lifetime. There are legitimate reasons to do so, including charitable giving strategies where the capital gain is avoided entirely. But the default assumption that a gift is a gift and inheritance is inheritance, with no tax difference between them, costs families real money.

> ***Exception to know:*** *Inherited assets that are held in a retirement account (IRA, 401(k)) do not receive a stepped-up basis. The funds inside a retirement account have never been taxed — tax is deferred until withdrawal. When a beneficiary inherits a retirement account and takes distributions, those distributions are taxed as ordinary income at the beneficiary's tax rate. This is a different and often more significant tax consideration than capital gains on non-retirement assets.*

Retirement Accounts: The Inheritance Rules Most Families Get Wrong

The rules governing how inherited retirement accounts are taxed changed significantly with the SECURE Act of 2019 and were further refined by subsequent legislation. Many families and some financial advisors are still operating under the old rules, which no longer apply to most beneficiaries.

Under the old rules, a non-spouse beneficiary who inherited an IRA could stretch required minimum distributions over their own life expectancy taking small amounts each year and allowing the rest to continue growing tax-deferred for decades. A 40- year-old who inherited a $500,000 IRA could take distributions over 40 or more years, managing the tax hit gradually.

That strategy called the stretch IRA is largely gone for most beneficiaries. Under current law, most non-spouse beneficiaries must withdraw the entire inherited retirement account within 10 years of the year of death. There are no required annual minimums within those 10 years, but the entire account must be empty by the end of year 10.

Who Inherits	Distribution Rules	Key Consideration
Surviving spouse	Can roll over to own IRA and delay RMDs until their own age 73	Most flexible option — treated as own account
Minor child of the deceased	10-year rule starts when child reaches age 21	Special rule ends at age of majority; then 10-year clock runs

Disabled or chronically ill individual	May stretch distributions over their own life expectancy	Must qualify under IRS definition at time of death
Person not more than 10 years younger	May use life expectancy method (the old stretch rule)	Applies to siblings, some older beneficiaries
All other non-spouse beneficiaries (most adult children)	Must withdraw entire account within 10 years of the year of death	No more lifetime stretch — tax planning within the 10 years is critical

The 10-year rule has significant tax implications that families need to plan around rather than discover at the worst possible time.

The tax compression problem

If a beneficiary inherits a $400,000 IRA and withdraws nothing for nine years, they must take the entire $400,000 in year 10. Added to their own income, that withdrawal may push them into a significantly higher tax bracket for that year paying far more in taxes than they would have if they had spread distributions strategically across all 10 years.

Beneficiaries who inherit retirement accounts under the 10-year rule should work with a tax advisor to develop a distribution strategy across the full decade taking larger distributions in lower-income years and smaller ones in higher-income years. This kind of planning can save thousands of dollars in taxes compared to taking an ad hoc approach.

Roth IRA inheritance

Roth IRAs follow the same 10-year rule for most non-spouse beneficiaries, with one critical difference: distributions from an inherited Roth IRA are generally tax-free, provided the account has been open for at least five years. A Roth IRA left to an adult child produces 10 years of tax-free growth and 10 years of tax-free withdrawals a significantly more valuable inheritance than the same dollar amount in a traditional IRA.

This difference in tax treatment is one argument for Roth conversions during your parent's lifetime, if they are in a lower tax bracket in retirement than their beneficiaries are likely to be. Converting a traditional IRA to a Roth means paying income tax now, during the conversion, in exchange for tax-free growth and tax-free distributions for the beneficiaries who inherit it. Whether a conversion makes sense depends on your parent's current and expected future tax rates, the size of the account, and the likely tax situation of the heirs.

When your parent is still taking RMDs

If your parent is over 73 and already taking required minimum distributions from retirement accounts, the year-of-death distribution matters. In the year your parent dies, they must take their RMD for that year if they haven't already. If your parent dies early in the year before taking the RMD, the beneficiary is responsible for taking that distribution before year end. Missing the year-of-death RMD triggers a penalty. This is one of the administrative details that gets missed in the chaos following a parent's death when no one has been briefed on it in advance.

Estate Taxes: What Most Families Don't Owe

Federal estate taxes generate significant anxiety among families who almost certainly will never owe them. The current federal estate tax exemption the amount an individual can pass to heirs free of federal estate tax is over $13 million per person as of this writing, with a married couple able to shelter more than $26 million combined through proper planning.

For most American families, federal estate tax is not a relevant concern. An estate worth $2 million, $5 million, even $8 million falls well below the federal threshold. The planning decisions covered in this book probate avoidance, long-term care protection, beneficiary designation management matter enormously for these families. Federal estate tax does not.

The important caveat: the current exemption levels are not permanent. They are set by legislation and scheduled to drop significantly unless Congress acts to extend them.

Families with estates approaching $5 million or more should monitor legislative developments and work with an estate planning attorney to ensure their plan remains optimal under different exemption scenarios.

State estate and inheritance taxes

While most families owe nothing in federal estate tax, state-level estate and inheritance taxes are a different matter. Twelve states and the District of Columbia impose their own estate taxes, several with exemptions well below the federal threshold.

Massachusetts, for example, taxes estates above $2 million. Oregon taxes above $1 million. The rates and structures vary significantly.

Separately, six states impose inheritance taxes paid by the beneficiary rather than the estate, based on the value of what they receive and their relationship to the deceased. Children generally pay lower rates or are exempt; more distant relatives pay higher rates.

If your parent lives in or owns property in one of these states, state-level estate or inheritance tax may be a real planning consideration even when federal tax is not. An elder law attorney in your parent's state can advise on the specific exposure and any available planning strategies.

> **Check your state:** The Tax Foundation maintains a regularly updated map showing which states have estate or inheritance taxes and their current thresholds. Search "state estate tax map" to find it. If your parent's state is on the list, include state tax planning in the attorney conversation.

Gifting Strategies: What Works and What Doesn't

Lifetime gifting can be a legitimate and effective part of an estate plan — reducing the taxable estate, helping family members when it matters most, and allowing your parent to see the impact of their generosity. But gifting decisions interact with Medicaid rules, capital gains rules, and gift tax rules in ways that require careful thought.

The annual gift exclusion

Each year, your parent can give up to a set amount per recipient without any gift tax consequences and without reducing their lifetime exemption. As of 2024, the annual exclusion is $18,000 per recipient. A parent with three adult children can give $18,000 to each — $54,000 total — in a single year without any reporting requirement and without touching the lifetime exemption. A married couple can give $36,000 per recipient per year by combining their exclusions through gift splitting.

Annual exclusion gifting is the most straightforward gifting strategy and works well as part of a long-term wealth transfer plan. It does not trigger the Medicaid lookback penalty provided the gifts are consistent with past patterns of gifting — though large or sudden increases in gifting around the time of a Medicaid application can draw scrutiny.

Direct payment of tuition and medical expenses

Payments made directly to an educational institution for tuition, or directly to a medical provider for healthcare expenses, are fully excluded from gift tax with no dollar limit.

Your parent can pay a grandchild's college tuition directly to the university and owe no gift tax on any amount, regardless of size, provided the payment goes directly to the institution and not to the grandchild. This is an often-underused gifting strategy for families with meaningful assets and grandchildren in education.

529 plan contributions

Your parent can contribute to a 529 college savings plan for a grandchild and elect to treat the contribution as if it were spread over five years for gift tax purposes — a strategy called super funding. This allows a single contribution of up to $90,000 (five times the annual exclusion) per beneficiary without gift tax consequences, provided no additional gifts to that beneficiary are made during the five-year period. A couple can superfund $180,000 per grandchild.

What to avoid

Large gifts of appreciated assets to avoid estate taxes can backfire through the capital gains mechanism described earlier in this chapter. Gifts made within five years of a Medicaid application are subject to the lookback penalty. Gifts that leave your parent without sufficient assets for their own care needs — essentially giving away their financial security prematurely — are a mistake that no amount of tax savings justifies. Your parent's financial security comes before their children's inheritance. That is a Ramsey principle as much as it is a planning principle.

> *Generosity is a virtue. Generosity that leaves your parents unable to fund their own care is a mistake. Plan the gifting around the security first.*

Coordinating the Plan: Putting It All Together

The decisions in this chapter do not live in isolation. Beneficiary designations interact with the trust. The stepped-up basis calculation affects whether to gift assets or hold them in the estate. Retirement account distribution planning affects the beneficiaries' tax situation for a decade after the parent's death. State tax considerations affect how the overall plan is structured.

This is the level of detail where a generalist who read a few articles online becomes genuinely dangerous, and where an experienced estate planning or elder law attorney earns their fee. Not because the concepts are impossibly complex — this chapter has covered them in plain English — but because the interactions between them require a complete picture of your parent's specific assets, family situation, state of residence, and goals.

The checklist for this chapter is specific and actionable. Pull every beneficiary designation on file. Review the stepped-up basis implications for any assets your parent is considering giving away. Understand the 10-year rule and build a distribution strategy for any retirement accounts that will be inherited. Find out whether your parent's state has its own estate or inheritance tax. And bring all of this into the conversation with the estate planning attorney rather than treating each piece as a separate question.

These details are the difference between a plan that works on paper and one that actually accomplishes what your parent intended when the time comes.

The Paperwork That Costs the Most

Nobody sits down to make the mistakes covered in this chapter. The ex-spouse who inherits the IRA was named on a form filled out 25 years ago. The minor grandchild who receives a lump sum at 18 was named with the best of intentions by someone who didn't know the alternative. The family that owes $36,000 in capital gains tax on an inherited stock portfolio didn't know they could have avoided it entirely.

These are not failures of character. They are failures of information, compounded by inertia. The family that reviews beneficiary designations annually, understands the stepped-up basis rule, and has talked to an advisor about retirement account distribution strategy will not make these mistakes. The family that treats these as administrative details not worth their time will.

Part Four moves into the situations that are genuinely complicated: cognitive decline, elder financial fraud, blended families, and special needs dependents. These are the chapters for families whose situation has specific complications that the standard planning framework doesn't fully address. Chapter 11 starts where urgency lives — what to do when cognitive decline has already begun.

PART FOUR: WHEN IT'S COMPLICATED

Cognitive Decline, Blended Families, and Difficult Situations

CHAPTER 11

Racing the Clock: What to Do When Cognitive Decline Has Already Started

The window for planning closes faster than most families expect. This chapter is for families who have noticed something — who are watching a parent change — and who need to understand what is still possible, what urgency looks like, and what to do right now.

The Conversation Nobody Wants to Name

Most families know something is wrong before they say it out loud. There is a shift in how a parent handles a conversation, a bill, a familiar task. Repetition that didn't used to be there. Confusion that is easy to explain away once, twice, a third time — until the pattern becomes too consistent to ignore.

The instinct in these situations is often to wait. Wait for a formal diagnosis. Wait until it gets worse. Wait until there is no longer any ambiguity. The problem is that waiting has a direct cost in this specific situation — because the ability to sign legal documents depends on a standard called legal capacity, and that window narrows as cognitive decline progresses. By the time a family has waited for certainty, they may have waited past the point where the most important planning decisions can be made cleanly and legally.

This chapter is for families in that space: the period between noticing something and certainty, when the urgency is real even if the diagnosis isn't final. It is also for families who are past that point — who have a diagnosed parent and are trying to understand what options remain.

There is honest news on both sides. If you've noticed something but have not yet reached an advanced stage, there is probably still time to act — but not indefinitely. If your parent has already lost legal capacity, some options are closed, but others are not, and knowing which is which matters.

Legal Capacity: What It Is and What It Isn't

Legal capacity is not the same thing as a medical diagnosis. This distinction is one of the most important and most misunderstood facts in this entire area of planning.

A diagnosis of early Alzheimer's does not mean your parent lacks legal capacity to sign documents. A diagnosis of mild cognitive impairment does not mean they cannot execute a will or a durable power of attorney. Conversely, a parent who has not yet been formally diagnosed may nevertheless lack the legal capacity required for a specific document on a specific day, depending on how their cognition fluctuates.

Legal capacity is assessed at a specific point in time, for a specific type of decision. The standard varies by document type, but the core question is whether your parent understands the nature and consequences of what they are signing at the moment they sign it.

Legal Capacity	Medical Diagnosis
A legal standard — the ability to understand and appreciate the nature and consequences of a decision	A medical determination — the presence of a condition affecting cognitive function
Assessed at a specific point in time, for a specific type of decision	A clinical finding that may be progressive but does not have a fixed legal meaning
A person with early dementia may still have full legal capacity	A formal dementia diagnosis does not automatically mean legal incapacity
Can be document-specific: a person may have capacity to sign a healthcare directive but not a complex trust amendment	Is not document-specific: a diagnosis applies to the person, not to what they are being asked to sign

Determined by the attorney at the time of signing, with physician input if needed	Determined by a physician, neuropsychologist, or geriatrician through clinical evaluation

The practical implication of this distinction is significant: a parent in the early stages of cognitive decline may still have full legal capacity to execute estate planning documents, provided the signing happens during a clear period, with proper documentation, and with an attorney who specifically assesses capacity at the time of signing.

Waiting for a formal diagnosis before acting is often the wrong approach. Acting as soon as the concern exists — before capacity becomes questionable produces documents that are legally cleaner, harder to challenge, and more likely to reflect your parent's genuine wishes.

> *A document signed while capacity is intact and properly documented is far harder to challenge later than one signed under ambiguous circumstances — or not signed at all.*

Recognizing the Warning Signs

Families often struggle to distinguish between normal aging and the early signs of cognitive decline. The table below separates early warning signs which suggest the planning window is still open but narrowing from urgent warning signs that indicate the window may be closing faster than anticipated.

Early Warning Signs	Urgent Warning Signs
Repeating the same question or story within a single conversation	Confusion about the current year, month, or season
Difficulty finding words that were previously easy	Not recognizing familiar people or places
Forgetting recent events while remembering distant past clearly	Significant personality or behavioral changes
Difficulty managing finances that were previously handled well	Getting lost in familiar areas

Missing appointments or forgetting to pay bills	Inability to follow a conversation or track a simple sequence of events
Increased confusion in unfamiliar environments or situations	Making significant financial decisions without apparent understanding of consequences

Normal aging involves some slowing of processing speed, occasional word-finding difficulty, and minor memory lapses. What distinguishes cognitive decline is pattern, frequency, and impact on function. One forgotten name is unremarkable. Consistently forgetting names of people your parent has known for decades is a signal. Difficulty managing finances that were previously handled with ease is a signal. Getting disoriented in familiar places is a signal.

If you are seeing early warning signs, the appropriate response is not alarm — it is movement. Get the planning conversation started. Engage an elder law attorney. Get a cognitive assessment from the primary care physician. None of these steps commit you to any particular course of action, but they give you information and they preserve options.

> ***First step:*** *If you have noticed warning signs, call an elder law attorney this week — not to sign documents yet, but to have a consultation about what documents are needed, what the capacity assessment process looks like, and how much time you likely have to work with.*

The Window That Closes Faster Than Families Expect

Cognitive decline does not follow a predictable schedule. Some people remain in the mild stage for years. Others move from early signs to significant impairment in a matter of months. A hospitalization, an infection, a medication change, or a surgery can accelerate decline in ways that catch families completely off guard.

The planning window is the period during which your parents have sufficient legal capacity to execute the documents that will govern their affairs: the durable power of attorney, the healthcare directive, the living trust, the will. Once that window closes, your parent no longer has the legal capacity to execute those documents — the family loses the ability to create them voluntarily and is forced into the court-supervised alternative.

This is why timing is everything in this chapter. Every month that passes without action is a month of the window used up. A family that acts when they first notice something typically has enough time to do the planning properly. A family that waits for certainty before acting often does not.

The documents most urgent to execute

Not all documents carry equal urgency when time is a factor. The durable power of attorney and the healthcare directive are the most immediately critical they are also among the simpler documents to execute, require less legal complexity than a full trust, and provide the most immediate protection if your parent's condition deteriorates rapidly.

A living trust and pour-over will are important and should be done as part of the same process, but if your parent's situation is genuinely urgent and the attorney cannot complete everything at once, prioritize the DPOA and healthcare directive. A trust without a DPOA leaves a gap during incapacity. A DPOA without a trust means the estate may go through probate, but the family has legal authority to manage finances during the illness. One situation is manageable. The other is a crisis.

Accelerated estate planning

Some elder law attorneys offer what amounts to an expedited process for families in this situation — a focused engagement designed to get the critical documents signed quickly while capacity is clearly intact, followed by a more thorough trust and planning process if time allows. If you explain to an attorney that you believe your parent's cognitive situation is time-sensitive, a good attorney will adjust their approach accordingly. What to avoid: online document services that cannot assess capacity, do not have an attorney present at signing, and cannot testify to your parent's state of mind at the time the documents were executed. Documents signed this way are legally valid in many circumstances, but they are also more vulnerable to challenge — and in a cognitive decline scenario, the risk of a future challenge is real.

How a Qualified Attorney Assesses Capacity

A competent estate planning or elder law attorney does not simply hand documents to a client and collect signatures. When there is any question about a client's cognitive state, the attorney's job includes assessing whether the client has sufficient legal capacity to execute the documents in question.

This assessment typically involves meeting with the client privately without family members present to have a direct conversation. The attorney asks questions designed to evaluate whether the client understands what they are signing, who their family members are, the general nature of their assets, and the consequences of the document's provisions. An attorney who has this conversation and observes clear, consistent, rational responses has a strong basis for proceeding. An attorney who observes significant confusion, inability to answer basic orientation questions, or an apparent lack of understanding of what is being signed has a basis for slowing down.

The private meeting without family present is important for another reason: it allows the attorney to assess whether your parent is expressing their own genuine wishes or is being coached or pressured by a family member. A parent who says different things alone with the attorney than they say in front of a family member is a warning sign of undue influence.

When physician involvement is appropriate

In situations where there is meaningful question about legal capacity, the attorney may request a letter from your parent's physician or a neuropsychologist confirming that the patient demonstrated decision-making capacity as of a specific date. This letter becomes part of the estate planning file and provides documentation if the documents are ever challenged.

A formal neuropsychological evaluation a comprehensive cognitive assessment administered by a specialist provides the most detailed and legally defensible documentation of cognitive function at a specific point in time. These evaluations take several hours and assess memory, language, executive function, attention, and other cognitive domains. The results can be used both to support the validity of documents signed around the time of the evaluation and to establish a cognitive baseline for monitoring future changes.

Not every situation requires a formal neuropsychological evaluation. Many do not. But when there is genuine uncertainty about capacity, or when the family anticipates that a disgruntled heir might challenge the documents later, the investment in comprehensive documentation is worthwhile.

> ***Documentation principle:*** *The more contested the family dynamics, and the more significant the cognitive concern, the more thoroughly the capacity assessment and documentation process should be. A well-documented signing is far harder to challenge than one that relied on the assumption that everything was fine.*

Video Documentation: A Practical Protective Tool

One approach that has gained traction among elder law attorneys dealing with cognitive decline situations is video documentation of the signing process. With your parents' consent and the attorney's guidance, the document signing is recorded on video. The recording captures the attorney's capacity assessment questions, your parents' responses, and their acknowledgment of what they are signing and why.

A video of a person who is clearly oriented, articulate, and expressly confirming their wishes is a powerful piece of evidence if anyone later claims the person lacked capacity or was unduly influenced. It is significantly harder to mount a successful challenge against a document supported by that kind of documentation than against one supported only by the attorney's notes.

Not all attorneys offer this option, and not all families are comfortable with it. But for situations where the family dynamics suggest a future challenge is possible, and where the parent's cognitive situation makes capacity a genuine question, video documentation is worth discussing with the attorney.

If It May Already Be Too Late: What Options Remain

Some families reading this chapter are past the planning window. Their parent has a late-stage dementia diagnosis, is no longer able to meaningfully engage with legal documents, and clearly lacks the legal capacity required to execute a will, trust, or power of attorney. The options narrow significantly at this point, but they do not disappear entirely.

Conservatorship and guardianship

When a person lacks legal capacity and has no valid power of attorney or healthcare directive in place, the family's path forward is a court petition for conservatorship (financial management) and guardianship (personal and medical decisions). As Chapter 6 described in the context of the stroke scenario, this process is expensive, time-consuming, and puts the court in control of who is appointed. But it is the legal mechanism that exists precisely for this situation, and for families without other options, it is the right path even with its costs and limitations.

The conservatorship or guardianship petition should be filed as promptly as possible once it is clear that legal capacity is absent. Every month of delay without legal authority to manage finances is a month during which bills may go unpaid, financial exploitation may go unchecked, and medical decisions may be made without clear legal authority.

Joint account access

If your parents added you as a joint account holder on bank accounts while they were capable, you have legal access to those accounts without a court order. This provides some financial management capability in the absence of a DPOA. It is not a substitute for a joint account holder is not a DPOA agent and does not have the same breadth of authority but it prevents the most immediate financial management crisis while the conservatorship process proceeds.

Social Security representative payee

If your parent receives Social Security benefits and can no longer manage those funds, you can apply to the Social Security Administration to become their representative payee — the person authorized to receive and manage their Social Security income on their behalf. This is a separate process from conservatorship and does not require court involvement, though it does require SSA approval and imposes its own reporting requirements.

Assets that may already be protected

Even when estate planning documents cannot be created, some assets may already be positioned to transfer cleanly. Life insurance and retirement accounts with beneficiaries named beneficiaries transfer by designation and do not require court involvement. Accounts with payable-on-death designations transfer directly. A home that is jointly owned transfers to the surviving owner automatically.

Taking inventory of how existing assets are titled and designated — the work covered in Chapter 7 — becomes even more urgent in this situation, because understanding what will transfer cleanly and what will go through probate helps the family plan for what comes next.

> ***Critical point:*** *If your parent has any remaining clarity — any period of sufficient cognition, even brief — and there is a document they could sign that would meaningfully improve the family's situation, consult an elder law attorney immediately. Good days can be used, with proper documentation, to execute documents during a period of clarity even when overall capacity is diminished. An attorney who specializes in this area knows how to navigate these situations within the bounds of the law.*

Managing Family Dynamics During Cognitive Decline

Cognitive decline in a parent does something to families that is hard to predict until you're in it. It concentrates the family's attention on a single person and a single set of decisions in a way that surfaces every unresolved dynamic who has been present, who has been absent, who is trusted, who is not, whose judgment is valued, whose is dismissed.

The sibling who has been managing day-to-day care may feel that their judgment should carry more weight than a sibling who visits occasionally. The siblings who lives far away may feel excluded from decisions being made without their input. A parent who is still capable at some moments may be expressing preferences that different children interpret differently.

The principles from Chapter 3 apply here with added urgency. Transparency matters more, not less, when the situation is emotionally charged. Keeping all siblings informed through written updates, shared medical information with appropriate HIPAA authorizations, and documented decision-making reduces the grounds for conflict later. It does not guarantee harmony. But it eliminates the factual disputes that give conflict its fuel.

If the family dynamics are already contentious enough that you anticipate disputes about your parent's care or finances, engaging a geriatric care manager a professional who specializes in coordinating care for aging adults can provide neutral expertise and documentation. Their assessments carry weight that a family member's assertions do not, and their involvement signals that decisions are being made professionally rather than unilaterally.

The Ongoing Monitoring Responsibility

Once estate planning documents are in place for a parent with cognitive decline, the work is not over. Legal capacity can change. A parent who had capacity when documents were signed may lose it. Documents that were appropriate at the time of signing may need to be updated as the parent's situation evolves. The successor trustee and DPOA agent need to be ready to step in at the appropriate moment, and they need to know what that moment looks like.

Monitoring financial accounts for unusual transactions is particularly important. A parent with cognitive decline who retains some financial access is a potential exploitation target, both from outside scammers and from family members with access. Chapter 12 covers financial exploitation in detail, but the monitoring principle belongs here too: regular review of account statements, automatic alert systems for large transactions, and a clear understanding of who has access to what are all part of responsible stewardship when a parent's cognitive situation is compromised. Document everything. Conversations about financial decisions, care decisions, and your parent's expressed preferences documented in writing at the time they occur create a record that protects everyone involved if decisions are later questioned. This is not paranoia. It is responsible practice in a situation where ambiguity is inevitable and disputes are possible.

Acting Before the Window Closes

The families who navigate cognitive decline with the least damage legal, financial, and relational are almost universally the ones who acted early. Not because they knew exactly what was coming. Not because they had perfect information. But when they noticed something, they took it seriously enough to pick up the phone and call an attorney.

That call, made early, creates options. Made late, it finds that options have narrowed. Not made at all, it leaves the family in a court process that a one-hour attorney consultation might have prevented entirely. If something has felt off about your parents' cognition, trust that instinct enough to act on it. The cost of a consultation you didn't need is an hour of your time. The cost of a consultation that came too late can be measured in months of court proceedings and tens of thousands of dollars. Chapter 12 turns to a threat that often accompanies cognitive vulnerability: elder financial fraud, and specifically the version that comes from inside the family.

CHAPTER 12

Elder Financial Fraud: The Threat Inside and Outside the Family

Seniors are the primary target of financial exploitation in the United States. The most devastating version of that exploitation often comes not from strangers, but from people the parent trusts most. This chapter covers how to recognize it, how to stop it, and how to build an estate plan that makes it structurally difficult in the first place.

Why Seniors Are the Primary Target

Elder financial exploitation is not a niche problem. It is one of the most prevalent forms of financial crime in the country, with estimates of annual losses to seniors ranging from $3 billion to over $36 billion depending on how exploitation is defined and measured. The wide range reflects how much goes unreported because victims are often unaware, embarrassed, cognitively impaired, or dependent on the person who exploited them.

Seniors are targeted for reasons that have nothing to do with weakness and everything to do with circumstances. They tend to have accumulated assets over a lifetime. They often live alone or in relative isolation. They may have cognitive vulnerabilities that affect judgment. They are frequently trusting from a generation that extended trust more readily. And they are often dependent on others for care, which creates leverage that a bad actor can exploit.

The fraud takes two broad forms. External fraud comes from strangers: phone scams, romance scams, Medicare fraud, home repair scams, investment fraud, and an increasingly sophisticated range of online and phone-based schemes that target seniors specifically. Internal exploitation comes from people already in the parent's life family members, caregivers, neighbors, or anyone with existing access and trust.

External fraud is damaging. Internal exploitation is often catastrophic, because by the time it is discovered, it has typically been ongoing for months or years, the amounts involved are large, and recovery is difficult.

> *The hardest version of this conversation is not about a stranger who called with a scam. It's about the person in the family who slowly became a predator. That conversation needs to happen anyway.*

How Internal Exploitation Happens

Internal financial exploitation rarely begins with a calculated decision to steal. More often it begins with access a family member who starts managing finances during an illness, a caregiver who is given a debit card "for groceries," a trusted child who handles the checkbook because it's easier — and then gradually expands that access in ways that serve their own interests.

The escalation is typically slow enough that no single step triggers alarm. A small transfer. A loan that was always going to be paid back. A gift that the parent agreed to but may not have fully understood. Payments are characterized as compensation for caregiving that are well above market rate. By the time the pattern is visible, the total taken is often substantial and the trail is muddied by the relationship. Several factors make older adults particularly vulnerable to internal exploitation from family members specifically.

Cognitive decline

A parent whose memory and judgment are compromised may not notice that transactions are occurring, may not remember what they agreed to, and may be persuaded to authorize transfers they would never have approved of in full health. The exploiting family member may genuinely believe they are just "advancing" their inheritance or being compensated for caregiving a rationalization that does not make the behavior legal or ethical, but that explains how it begins.

Emotional dependency

A parent who is isolated, lonely, or heavily dependent on one person for daily care may tolerate or enable financial exploitation out of fear that confronting it will cost them their primary relationship. The exploiting person may explicitly or implicitly threaten withdrawal of care or affection, creating a dynamic where the parent feels they have no safe alternative.

Shame and secrecy

Many older adults who realize they are being exploited by a family member do not report it — not to other family members, not to authorities, not to anyone. The shame of admitting that a child or grandchild has been stealing from them, and the fear of what reporting it might do to the family, keeps the exploitation hidden and ongoing.

Misplaced trust in legal authority

A family member who holds a durable power of attorney, serves as a trustee, or has been named as a representative payee has legal authority over assets. That authority, misused, is not inherently more visible than unauthorized access — especially if no one else is monitoring the accounts or reviewing the accountings. Legal authority without oversight is the condition that enables the most large-scale exploitation.

Warning Signs: What to Look For

Recognizing internal exploitation requires paying attention to both financial patterns and behavioral changes. The table below covers the most consistent warning signs across both dimensions.

Financial Warning Signs	Behavioral Warning Signs
Unexplained withdrawals or transfers from bank accounts	A new "best friend" or companion who seems overly interested in finances
Unpaid bills despite adequate income or savings	Isolation from friends and other family members
Changes to wills, trusts, or beneficiary designations that the parent cannot explain	Fear, anxiety, or unusual deference in the presence of a specific person
Signatures on documents that the parent doesn't remember signing	Reluctance to speak freely when certain people are present
Large gifts or loans to a caregiver, family member, or new acquaintance	Sudden changes in attitude toward family members who were previously close
Missing financial statements, account books, or legal documents	Confusion about financial decisions they've apparently already made
A power of attorney agent who refuses to provide accountings or information	New person accompanying the parent to all medical and legal appointments

The most reliable single indicator is a change that cannot be explained by your parent's own choices made in full understanding. When financial changes occur in the context of cognitive decline, isolation, or a specific person's increasing control over your parent's life, the combination warrants serious attention.

The hardest warning sign to act on is often the behavioral one: a parent who seems afraid or overly deferential in the presence of a specific person, or who seems to have changed their relationship with other family members suddenly and without explanation. These are often signs of a dynamic that has already advanced well beyond the early stages.

External Scams: The Ones That Target Seniors Specifically

While internal exploitation causes the most damage per incident, external scams reach a far larger number of seniors. Understanding the most prevalent ones helps families recognize them before they cause damage and helps parents understand why certain contacts and requests are worth immediate skepticism.

The grandparent scam

A caller claims to be a grandchild in trouble arrested, hospitalized, stranded in a foreign country and urgently needs money wired immediately. The caller instructs the target not to tell other family members because of embarrassment. A second caller, posing as an attorney or law enforcement officer, reinforces the urgency. The combination of fabricated emergencies, emotional manipulation, and secrecy pressure has cost seniors hundreds of thousands of dollars per incident. The defense is simple: hang up and call the grandchild directly on a known number.

The romance scam

A relationship develops online or by phone with someone the senior has never met in person. Over weeks or months, the relationship deepens. Then a crisis occurs a medical emergency, a business opportunity, a stranded travel situation and money is needed urgently. By the time families discover it, the emotional investment is significant, and the financial losses often are too. Romance scams cause some of the largest individual losses of any senior fraud category and are among the most psychologically damaging.

Medicare and Social Security scams

Callers claim to represent Medicare or the Social Security Administration and warn of benefit suspension, overpayment recovery, or account verification requirements. They request Social

Security numbers, banking information, or payment. Neither Medicare nor Social Security will call to demand immediate payment or threaten benefit suspension by phone. Any such call should be hung up immediately and reported to 1- 800-MEDICARE or the SSA's fraud hotline.

Home repair and contractor fraud

An unsolicited contractor offers dramatically discounted repairs or spots a "serious problem" that requires immediate attention. They collect a large upfront payment and either disappear, do minimal work, or create additional "problems" requiring further payment. Seniors living alone are disproportionately targeted. The defense is to require written estimates from multiple contractors, never pay in full upfront, and verify licensure with the state contractor licensing board before any work begins.

Investment and lottery fraud

Guaranteed high returns, unclaimed prize winnings that require a fee to collect, cryptocurrency investment opportunities all of these exploit the combination of asset accumulation and sometimes reduced skepticism that makes seniors a prime target for investment fraud. The foundational rule applies universally: if someone is calling you to offer a financial opportunity you didn't seek out, it is almost certainly a scam.

> ***Practical protection:*** *Set up a code word with your parent that any legitimate family emergency call must include. If a caller claiming to be a grandchild in trouble cannot provide the code word, it's a scam. This simple measure stops the grandparent scam entirely.*

How a Properly Structured Trust Protects a Vulnerable Parent

The most powerful protection against both internal and external financial exploitation is structural — built into the estate plan itself rather than relying on vigilance, trust, or the goodwill of individuals with access.

A well-drafted revocable living trust can include provisions that create accountability by design. The table below covers the most effective structural protections and how each one works.

Protection	How It Works
Co-trustee requirement	Two signatures required for transactions above a set threshold — makes unauthorized transfers structurally impossible without co-trustee involvement
Mandatory accounting provisions	Trust requires regular accountings sent to all beneficiaries — irregularities become visible before they compound
Independent trustee for specific assets	A corporate or professional trustee manages certain assets, removing them from a family member's sole control
Transaction alert thresholds	Bank account alerts notify designated family members of transactions above a set dollar amount — early warning system outside the trust structure
Restricted DPOA authority	DPOA drafted with specific exclusions — agent cannot make gifts, change beneficiaries, or benefit themselves above compensation limits
Annual independent review	CPA or financial advisor reviews accounts annually and reports findings to all beneficiaries — independent eyes on the numbers

These protections are not boilerplate. They require deliberate drafting instructions to the attorney and a clear conversation about the specific vulnerabilities the family is concerned about. An attorney who is told that a parent has cognitive vulnerabilities, that one family member has more access than others, or that there is a history of financial dysfunction in the family will draft differently than one who is not.

Be specific with your attorney about what you are worried about. That specificity is what produces a plan with real protective teeth rather than standard language that sounds protective but functions as a formality.

The DPOA Problem: Authority Without Accountability

The durable power of attorney is one of the most important protective documents in an estate plan, and it is also the instrument most frequently misused by exploiting family members. The reason is structural: a DPOA gives broad legal authority to a single person, and that authority is largely self-executing. The agent does not need to consult anyone, report to anyone, or justify their actions to anyone in the normal course of events.

An agent who decides to transfer funds to themselves, make gifts on their parent's behalf, or use the parent's assets for their own benefit may technically have the authority to do so under a broadly worded DPOA or may be acting outside their authority in ways that are difficult to detect and prove after the fact.

There are drafting choices that reduce this risk without rendering the DPOA unworkable. A DPOA can explicitly prohibit the agent from making gifts to themselves, changing beneficiary designations that benefit themselves, or taking compensation above a specified market rate. It can require the agent to provide annual accountings to other family members or a specified neutral party. It can name a monitor a third person whose role is specifically to review the agent's actions and raise concerns if something seems wrong.

These provisions will not prevent a determined bad actor who is willing to act outside the document's terms. But they make unauthorized action more difficult, more visible, and more clearly illegal if it occurs — which matters both as a deterrent and as a basis for legal action if exploitation is discovered.

> ***Choose the agent carefully:*** *The DPOA agent appointment is not a consolation prize for a family member who didn't get the executor role. It is a position of real authority over real assets, granted to a person who will operate largely without supervision. The qualities that matter are honesty, financial competence, and the ability to act in your parent's interest rather than their own. If no family member meets that bar confidently, a professional fiduciary is a legitimate alternative.*

What to Do If You Suspect Exploitation Is Already Happening

This is the section that most books on this topic handle too gently. So here it is plainly: if you have credible reason to believe a family member is financially exploiting your parent, this is not a situation to handle through a family conversation first.

A family confrontation alerts the exploiting person, gives them the opportunity to cover tracks, move assets, destroy records, or increase their isolation of the parent. Families that approach suspected exploitation as a communication problem to be resolved around a kitchen table often find that by the time the legal process catches up, the assets are gone and the documentation is gone with them.

The right sequence is legal and institutional, not interpersonal.

Step one: Document what you know

Before contacting anyone, gather what evidence is available. Bank statements, transfer records, account changes, documents that were signed, photographs of any relevant paperwork. Do this quietly and without alerting the suspected exploiter. What you gather becomes the foundation of any legal action or regulatory report.

Step two: Contact an elder law attorney

An elder law attorney with experience in exploitation cases can advise on the legal options available given your parent's specific situation and state. Options may include seeking emergency conservatorship or guardianship to remove the exploiting person's legal access to your parent's finances, filing a civil lawsuit to recover misappropriated assets, or working with law enforcement on a criminal referral.

Do not engage the family attorney who has an existing relationship with the exploiting family member. Engage an independent attorney who has no prior relationship with any party.

Step three: Report to Adult Protective Services

Every state has an Adult Protective Services (APS) agency that receives reports of elder abuse and financial exploitation. APS can investigate, has authority to intervene, and can coordinate with law enforcement. Reports can typically be made by phone or online, and reporters are generally protected from retaliation.

APS does not always move quickly, and their authority is limited to certain circumstances. But a filed report creates an official record, triggers a formal investigation, and puts the situation on record with an agency that has statutory authority to act.

Step four: Contact financial institutions

Banks and credit unions have increasing legal authority and obligation to flag and freeze accounts where elder financial exploitation is suspected. Many states have laws specifically authorizing financial institutions to place temporary holds on accounts when exploitation is reported. Contact the financial institution's fraud or elder care department and explain what you have observed. Provide documentation if you have it.

Step five: Consider law enforcement

Financial exploitation of an elder is a crime in every state. The severity of the charge and the likelihood of prosecution varies by state, the amount involved, and the specific conduct. Law enforcement referrals are most likely to result in prosecution when there is clear documentation of unauthorized transactions, the amount is significant, and there is a paper trail that distinguishes unauthorized exploitation from authorized but contested decisions.

> ***When the parent refuses help:*** *A parent who is being exploited may refuse to acknowledge it, refuse to cooperate with efforts to stop it, or actively defend the exploiting person. This is common, painful, and legally complicated. An adult who retains legal capacity has the right to make bad decisions, including the decision to continue a relationship with someone who is exploiting them. When this situation occurs, the focus shifts to protecting whatever assets can be protected and ensuring the parent has access to independent information and support, while respecting their legal autonomy. An elder law attorney can advise on the specific options available.*

Prevention: The Conversations Worth Having Now

The best protection against elder financial exploitation is a combination of structural safeguards built into the estate plan and an informed, connected family that pays attention to the warning signs.

Talk to your parents explicitly about the most common scams targeting seniors. Not as a warning that they're vulnerable — most seniors find that framing condescending but as information that is relevant to everyone. The grandparent scam, the Medicare scam, the romance scam: these are worth naming and describing specifically. A parent who has heard of a scam is far less likely to fall for it than one who encounters it with no frame of reference.

Establish a family habit of transparency around finances. Not surveillance transparency. A parent who knows that other family members have some visibility into their financial situation, and who has agreed to that as part of a broader planning conversation, has a built-in check on exploitation from any direction.

And build the oversight into the estate plan itself, before a crisis makes it necessary. Co-trustee requirements, mandatory accountings, transaction alerts, restricted DPOA language these work best when they are established during a calm, forward-looking planning conversation, not retrofitted in response to suspected exploitation.

> ***One practical step:*** *Ask your parent if they would be willing to add you or another trusted family member to receive electronic statements from their bank accounts.*
> *Not to have access to the funds just to see the statements. That one visibility measure stops a significant percentage of internal exploitation before it progresses beyond early stages.*

Protection Is an Act of Love

Talking about elder financial exploitation in the context of your own family is uncomfortable. It requires naming, at least implicitly, that the threat might come from within. That is a hard thing to acknowledge about people you love.

But the families that protect their aging parents most effectively are the ones that take the threat seriously before it materializes, build the structural safeguards, have the conversations, and pay enough attention to notice when something is wrong. The discomfort of those conversations is real. The cost of not having them can be catastrophic.

A parent who has been financially exploited whether by a stranger or a family member loses not just money but trust, dignity, and sometimes their ability to fund their own care. Protecting against that outcome is not a bureaucratic exercise. It is one of the most concrete expressions of what it means to take care of someone.

Chapter 13 moves to blended families the dynamics that arise when second marriages, stepchildren, and competing family loyalties intersect with estate planning decisions that have to serve everyone fairly.

CHAPTER 13

Blended Families, Second Marriages, and Complicated Dynamics

A second marriage changes everything about estate planning. Without deliberate, specific planning, blended family dynamics produce outcomes that nobody intended and everyone regrets. This chapter covers what actually happens without a plan, the trust structures designed for this situation, and how to have the conversations that make all of it possible.

Why Standard Estate Planning Breaks Down in Blended Families

The standard estate planning framework assumes a relatively simple structure: one set of parents, one set of children, assets accumulated together over a shared lifetime. A revocable living trust with the spouse as primary beneficiary and the children as remainder beneficiaries. Clean lines. Shared goals. Straightforward distribution.

A blended family breaks every one of those assumptions. Assets may have been accumulated before the marriage and belong emotionally, if not legally, to one family line. The spouse and the children may have competing legitimate interests in those assets. The surviving spouse is both someone your parent loves and a potential barrier between your parent's biological children and an inheritance their parent intended them to receive. And the longer the second marriage lasts, the more those asset lines blur.

This is not a problem of bad intentions. Most step-parents are not scheming to divert assets from their stepchildren. Most biological children are not scheming to deprive a step-parent of a comfortable retirement. The conflict arises because a standard estate plan — drafted without explicit thought about the blended family dynamics — produces outcomes that look like scheming even when nobody intended anything of the sort.

The scenario from Chapter 6 illustrated this directly: a widower remarries, means to update his estate plan, dies before doing so, and leaves a situation where his new wife has rights that conflict with his biological children's expectations. No one was villainous. The absence of a deliberate plan created the conflict.

> *In a blended family, 'we'll figure it out when the time comes' is not a plan. It is a guaranteed family fracture in slow motion.*

What Happens Without a Plan in a Blended Family

The default outcomes produced by intestacy law and standard joint estate planning in blended families range from awkward to catastrophic. The table below maps the most common situations against what happens without deliberate planning and what the right plan produces instead.

Situation	Without a Plan	With the Right Plan
Parent dies; surviving spouse is a step-parent	Step-parent inherits everything. Biological children may get nothing until step-parent dies — if ever.	QTIP or bypass trust ensures step-parent is cared for while protecting biological children's inheritance.
Step-parent dies first; leaves assets to own children	Biological children watch assets their parent accumulated pass to a step- sibling family instead.	Trust specifies which assets belong to which family line and controls distribution accordingly.
Parent remarries; step-parent moves into family home	Home passes to step-parent at death. Step-parent may will it to their own children.	Life estate or trust specifies step-parent's right to remain; home then passes to biological children.
Parent names step-parent as sole DPOA and trustee	Step-parent controls all financial decisions during incapacity; biological children have no visibility.	Co-trustee structure or independent trustee provides oversight; biological children receive accountings.

Parent dies intestate (no plan at all)	State intestacy law distributes assets — usually to spouse first, which in many states means the step-parent receives the bulk.	Any documented plan is better than intestacy. A trust removes state law from the equation entirely.

The pattern is consistent: without planning that specifically addresses the blended family structure, the law defaults to protecting the surviving spouse, which in practice often means biological children from the first marriage receive little or nothing until the step-parent also dies. And even then, what they receive depends entirely on what the step-parent chose to do with the assets during their own lifetime.

That outcome may or may not reflect what your parent actually wanted. The problem is that without a plan, nobody knows what they wanted — and the law fills the gap with its own defaults, not your parent's wishes.

The Core Tension: Protecting Two Legitimate Interests

The fundamental planning challenge in a second marriage is that two sets of people have legitimate competing interests in the same assets, and a good plan must serve both simultaneously.

The surviving spouse has a legitimate interest in financial security for the rest of their life. If they shared a household, contributed to its upkeep, and organized their own financial life around the expectation of joint resources, their need for continued access to those resources is real and reasonable. A plan that leaves a surviving spouse immediately impoverished to protect the biological children's inheritance is not a fair plan, and most parents do not want it.

The biological children have a legitimate interest in receiving the inheritance their parents intended for them — particularly assets that predated the second marriage, that were accumulated with or for them in mind, or that carry family significance beyond their dollar value. A plan that requires them to wait indefinitely, with no guarantee of what will be left, for a stepparent they may barely know is not a fair plan either.

The right planning tools are designed to serve both interests at the same time: providing the surviving spouse with financial security and, where appropriate, access to assets during their lifetime, while guaranteeing that the biological children receive what their parent intended at the step-parent's death. These tools exist specifically because this tension is common and the standard trust structure does not resolve it.

> ***The key principle:*** *Your parent's goal is not to choose between their spouse and their children. A properly structured plan provides for both. The question is how to draw the line between access and ownership in a way that everyone understands and has agreed to before anyone dies.*

Trust Structures Built for Blended Families

Several trust structures have been developed specifically to address the competing interests of surviving spouses and biological children from a prior marriage. Each makes a different set of trade-offs. Understanding them helps families ask the right questions when working with an estate planning attorney.

Trust Structure	How It Works	Best For
QTIP Trust (Qualified Terminable Interest Property)	Spouse receives all income from the trust during their lifetime. At the spouse's death, remaining assets pass to biological children.	Couples with significant assets where both spouse's care and children's inheritance need protection.
Bypass Trust (Credit Shelter Trust)	Assets up to the estate tax exemption pass into a trust at first death. Spouse has limited access; remainder goes to biological children at spouse's death.	Larger estates where tax planning and inheritance protection need to work simultaneously.

Separate Property Trust	Each spouse's pre-marital and separately acquired assets are held in their own trust, with independent beneficiary designations.	Couples who want to keep their financial lives more separate and pass pre-marital wealth directly to their own children.
Discretionary Trust with Independent Trustee	An independent trustee (professional or corporate) manages assets and makes distribution decisions according to written criteria, removing family conflict from the equation.	High-conflict blended families where no family member can serve as trustee without creating resentment.
Tenancy in Common with Specific Bequests	Real estate owned as tenancy in common (not joint tenancy) allows each spouse's share to pass per their individual will or trust rather than automatically to the survivor.	Protecting biological children's interest in a shared home without requiring full trust setup for smaller estates.

The QTIP Trust in practice

The Qualified Terminable Interest Property trust is the workhorse of blended family estate planning. When the first spouse dies, assets pour into the QTIP trust. The surviving spouse receives all income generated by the trust for the rest of their life — interest, dividends, rental income — and may have access to principal for health, education, maintenance, and support depending on how the trust is drafted. At the surviving spouse's death, whatever remains in the trust passes to the biological children of the first spouse.

The QTIP achieves the core goal: the surviving spouse cannot be left destitute, and the biological children cannot be disinherited. The step-parent gets income security. The biological children get the remainder. Neither can unilaterally change that outcome.

The trustee of a QTIP trust carries real responsibility — they manage assets for two parties with competing interests and must navigate principal distribution decisions carefully. An independent trustee — a professional or corporate fiduciary — is often the right choice for this role in high-conflict or high-value situations, because a family member serving as trustee will inevitably be perceived as favoring one side.

Separate property trusts and prenuptial agreements

For parents approaching or already in a second marriage with significant pre-marital assets, the cleaner solution is often to keep those assets legally separate from the beginning. A prenuptial agreement that identifies pre-marital assets as separate property, combined with a trust that holds those assets for the benefit of the biological children, removes them from the marital estate entirely. The surviving spouse has no claim on assets that were never part of the marital property.

This approach requires honesty and agreement before the marriage, which is why it is difficult but also why it works. Both spouses enter the marriage with clear understanding of what belongs to each family line. There is no ambiguity to exploit or dispute after a death.

A prenuptial agreement that was never executed is not a prenuptial agreement. Good intentions do not substitute for a signed document. If your parent is contemplating remarriage or is newly remarried without a prenuptial agreement, it is not too late to execute a postnuptial agreement, which serves the same function. The willingness to have that conversation itself revealing about whether both spouses share the same understanding of what the plan is.

The Family Home in a Blended Family

The family home is almost always the most emotionally loaded asset in a blended family estate plan, and it is the one where the conflict between the surviving spouse's need for security and the biological children's interest in inheritance is sharpest.

A step-parent who has lived in the home for 15 years, who organized their daily life around it, and who has nowhere else to go has a real claim to continue residence. Requiring them to vacate immediately so the biological children can sell is cruel and, in many states, legally restricted anyway through spousal protection statutes.

Biological children who grew up in the home, who watched their parents pay it off over decades, who see it as representing their parent's life work, have a real interest in ensuring it eventually comes to them rather than to a step-sibling family.

Both interests can be honored simultaneously through planning. A life estate deed or a properly structured trust can give the surviving step-parent the right to remain in the home for their lifetime or until remarriage or voluntary departure, after which the home passes to the biological children. The step-parent cannot sell the home or encumber it without the biological children's consent, which protects their remainder interest. The biological children cannot force the step-parent out, which protects the spouse's security.

The specific mechanics life estate, trust with life tenancy provisions, tenancy in common with will bequests depend on the state, the home's value, and the family's specific dynamics. An elder law attorney who understands the blended family context will know which instrument fits in which situation.

> ***The joint tenancy mistake:*** *Adding a new spouse as joint tenant with right of survivorship on the family home solves one problem — the home avoids probate at the first death — while creating a larger one. The step-parent now owns the home outright and can do whatever they choose with it, including willing it to their own children. Biological children have no enforceable claim. This is the mechanism behind many of the most painful blended family disputes, and it is entirely avoidable.*

Having the Conversation: With Your Parent and with the Blended Family

The technical planning solutions in this chapter are not difficult to implement. The difficult part is the conversation that has to happen before they can be implemented — the one where your parent and their spouse talk honestly about what each of them wants, what each family line's legitimate interests are, and how they want to resolve the inherent tensions.

That conversation requires your parent to say explicitly, to their spouse, something like: I love you and I want you to be secure for the rest of your life. I also want my children to receive what I've built for them. I want to find a plan that does both, and I need us to agree on what that looks like. That is an honest framing. It is also a vulnerable one, because it names the tension directly rather than leaving it buried under vague reassurances.

Some second spouses will engage with that conversation productively. They share the concern. They want the stepchildren to be treated fairly. They are willing to sign a prenuptial or postnuptial agreement, agree to a QTIP structure, or accept trustee oversight as reasonable under the circumstances. These conversations, while uncomfortable, end in documented agreements that protect everyone.

Other second spouses will resist any planning that they perceive as limiting their own authority over shared assets. They may frame the conversation as a sign of distrust, as the biological children trying to interfere in the marriage, or as unnecessary. This resistance is itself diagnostic information. A spouse who refuses to acknowledge the legitimate interests of biological children from a prior marriage is telling you something important about how they will exercise authority if they become the sole decision-maker.

> *A spouse who refuses to participate in blended family estate planning is not just avoiding paperwork. They are refusing to acknowledge that your parent's children have any legitimate claim on the future. That refusal should be taken seriously.*

What to Do When You're the Adult Child of the First Marriage

If you are reading this chapter as an adult child whose parent has remarried, your position in this planning process is delicate. You have real interests at stake, and those interests are legitimate. You also do not have authority over your parent's decisions, and any approach that comes across as controlling, suspicious, or adversarial toward the step-parent will make the conversation harder, not easier.

The most effective posture is collaborative. You are not trying to restrict your parent's choices. You are trying to help them create a plan that serves everyone they love — including their spouse — without leaving anything to chance. You want clarity, not control.

Questions worth raising with your parent

What happens to the house if you die first? What would you want your spouse to be able to do with it, and what would you want to happen to it eventually? Have you and your spouse talked about this? Does your spouse know what you're hoping for regarding what you pass to us?

These questions invite your parent into a forward-looking planning conversation rather than a backward-looking dispute. They surface the same planning gaps that an estate planning attorney would identify, but in the context of a family conversation rather than a legal one.

What to avoid

Framing the conversation as "I'm worried your spouse is going to take everything." Even if that worry is legitimate, leading with it puts your parent on the defensive and makes them choose between you and their spouse in a way that usually ends with you losing.

Going around your parent to engage directly with the estate planning attorney. The attorney represents your parent, not you. Attempting to influence the plan outside your parent's knowledge or consent is both ineffective and potentially damaging to the family relationship.

Waiting until your parent dies and then litigating. By that point, any assets that were going to be diverted have already been diverted, legal challenges are expensive and uncertain, and the relationship with the step-parent's family is permanently damaged. Prevention through planning is worth enormously more than litigation after the fact.

> ***If your parent will not engage:*** *And the step-parent situation genuinely concerns you — consult an elder law attorney privately, not to take action behind your parent's back, but to understand what your legal options are if your parent dies without a plan. Knowing the landscape in advance lets you respond quickly and appropriately if the situation deteriorates.*

When the Step-Parent Is the One Who Needs Protection

Not every blended family situation involves biological children worried about a step- parent. Sometimes the dynamic runs the other direction: a step-parent who contributed meaningfully to a household and to the care of a parent over many years, who has limited assets of their own, and whose financial security depends on access to the shared estate. In that situation, the planning challenge is ensuring the step-parent is genuinely protected rather than assuming that "everything to my children" is the right answer.

A parent who has a younger spouse, or a spouse who gave up a career to provide caregiving, or a spouse who sold their own home and assets to contribute to the shared household has created obligations that a thoughtful estate plan acknowledges. Leaving that spouse with nothing, or with a right to income from a trust that is inadequate for their actual needs, is neither fair nor what most parents want when they think it through carefully.

The QTIP trust and similar structures are designed to work in both directions — they protect both the spouse's income security and the biological children's remainder interest. The specific balance between the two — how much principal access the spouse has, under what conditions, and whether that access can erode what passes to the children — is the drafting decision that requires the most careful thought.

There is no universally right answer. What matters is that the answer chosen reflects your parent's genuine intentions, has been communicated clearly to both the spouse and the biological children, and is documented in a trust that will actually implement those intentions rather than leaving them as expressed wishes with no legal force.

The Annual Conversation That Prevents Surprises

One of the most effective tools in blended family estate planning is not a legal document. It is a regular, explicit conversation between your parent and both sides of the blended family about what the plan is and whether it still reflects everyone's understanding.

Many blended family conflicts erupt after a death because the biological children did not know what the plan was, the step-parent did not know what the biological children expected, and the parent who understood both sides never made their intentions explicit to anyone. Each party assumed the situation was being handled in a way that favored their interests. None of them were correct.

A parent who sits down periodically with their spouse and their biological children and says "here is the plan, here is what it provides for each of you, here is why we made these decisions" removes the ambiguity that conflict feeds on. The conversation may be uncomfortable. The discomfort of a living conversation is orders of magnitude less than the damage of a posthumous dispute.

Chapter 18 covers estate plan reviews in detail. For blended family situations specifically, any significant change in the relationship — a change in the step-parent's health or financial situation, a change in a biological child's circumstances, a significant change in the value of assets — warrants an immediate review of whether the plan still does what it was designed to do.

The Plan That Honors Everyone

Blended families are not planning problems to be minimized. They are families with real relationships, real histories, and real competing interests that deserve to be taken seriously and addressed honestly. The planning tools exist. The legal structures work. What requires the most effort is not the legal drafting but the human conversation that has to happen first.

A parent who has the courage to name the competing interests, sit with both sides of the family, and commit to a plan that they can explain and defend is giving everyone involved something rare: certainty. Not certainty that every outcome is perfect, but certainty about what the plan is and whose interests it serves and why.

That certainty is what prevents the disputes, the litigation, and the family fractures that make blended family estate failures so damaging. It is worth the uncomfortable conversation to achieve it.

Chapter 14 addresses a different set of complicated circumstances: families where a parent has a special needs dependent — a child or sibling with a disability — whose financial security is tied directly to how the estate plan is structured and whether government benefits are preserved or inadvertently destroyed by an inheritance.

CHAPTER 14

When a Parent Has Special Needs Dependents

A well-meaning inheritance can destroy a disabled family member's access to government benefits in a matter of weeks. The tools that prevent this outcome exist and work — but they require specific, deliberate planning. This chapter covers what those tools are, when they're needed, and what happens to families who don't use them.

The Inheritance That Helps and Then Hurts

A parent dies and leaves a portion of their estate to a child with a disability. The child receives an inheritance that the parent spent a lifetime accumulating and intended as an act of love and provision. Within months, that child's SSI payments stop. Their Medicaid coverage — which funds their medications, therapies, and in some cases their residential placement — is terminated. The family scrambles to spend down the inheritance fast enough to restore eligibility, often on things the disabled family member doesn't particularly need and would never have chosen, because the alternative is losing benefits that sustain their daily life.

This scenario happens repeatedly, to families who loved their disabled family member deeply and simply did not know that a direct inheritance would trigger this outcome. It is not an obscure edge case. It is the predictable result of leaving assets directly to anyone receiving means-tested government benefits, and it can be entirely prevented with a Special Needs Trust.

A Special Needs Trust — also called a Supplemental Needs Trust — is a legal structure that holds assets for the benefit of a person with a disability in a way that does not count as that person's own asset for government benefit eligibility purposes. The trust supplements government benefits rather than replacing them. The beneficiary keeps their SSI, their Medicaid, their housing assistance, and their program placements. They also benefit from the trust's assets — for things those government programs do not cover.

> *The goal of a Special Needs Trust is not to hide money from the government. It is to ensure that the people who love a disabled family*

member can provide for them without inadvertently destroying the benefits they depend on to survive.

Which Government Benefits Are at Risk

Not all government benefits are means-tested, and not all means-tested benefits are affected the same way by an inheritance. Understanding which programs are at risk — and how — determines how urgently a Special Needs Trust is needed and how it needs to be structured.

Government Program	Asset Limit	Direct Inheritance Impact	SNT Protects Benefits?
SSI (Supplemental Security Income)	$2,000 individual	Benefits suspended until inheritance is spent down to limit	Yes — SNT assets not counted
Medicaid (for individuals with disabilities)	Varies by state; typically very low	Eligibility terminated until assets spent down	Yes — SNT assets not counted
Section 8 Housing Assistance	Income and asset based	May affect eligibility or monthly contribution	Generally yes, depending on trust structure
Group home / residential program funding	Medicaid-based; low asset threshold	Medicaid termination disrupts residential placement and services	Yes — properly structured SNT preserves Medicaid

SSDI (Social Security Disability Insurance)	No asset limit	Direct inheritance does not affect SSDI	SNT still useful to protect Medicaid eligibility tied to SSDI

SSI and Medicaid are the two programs that create the most urgent need for a Special Needs Trust. Both have very low asset limits — SSI at $2,000 for an individual — and both are terminated when a beneficiary's countable assets exceed those limits. A direct inheritance of even a modest amount can disqualify a beneficiary immediately.

The disruption to Medicaid is often the most damaging. For a family member who relies on Medicaid for medications, therapies, medical equipment, home health aides, or a residential group home placement, losing Medicaid coverage is not an inconvenience. It is a crisis. Group home placements in particular may be lost — because the facility's funding depends on Medicaid — and waiting lists for those placements can be years long. Restoring the placement after Medicaid eligibility is reestablished may be impossible in practice even after the legal eligibility is technically restored.

> ***The spend-down trap:*** *Families who discover the problem after an inheritance has already been received sometimes assume they can quickly spend down the assets to restore eligibility. The spend-down has to be on legitimate, allowable expenditures — not gifts or transfers that trigger their own penalty periods. And the damage done during the ineligibility period — lost residential placements, interrupted therapies, lapsed medications — may be irreversible regardless of how quickly eligibility is restored.*

The Three Types of Special Needs Trusts

There are three main structures for a Special Needs Trust, and choosing the right one depends on where the assets in the trust are coming from, who is setting it up, and what the family's long-term goals are.

	First-Party SNT (d4A	Third-Party SNT	Pooled Trust

	Trust)		
Funded with	Beneficiary's own assets (personal injury settlement, inherited before trust existed)	Assets from someone else — parent, grandparent, estate	Assets pooled with other beneficiaries; managed by nonprofit
Who can create it	Beneficiary, parent, grandparent, legal guardian, or court	Anyone except the beneficiary	Nonprofit organization manages; family contributes
Medicaid payback at death?	Yes — state Medicaid reimbursed before any remainder passes to heirs	No — remainder passes to named beneficiaries	Partial — varies by nonprofit and trust terms
Best use	When beneficiary already received assets and needs to protect benefits retroactively	Estate planning — receiving inheritance, life insurance, or gifts without disrupting benefits	Smaller amounts where standalone trust cost isn't justified; good interim option

For estate planning purposes — a parent who wants to leave assets to a disabled child without disrupting their benefits — the Third-Party Special Needs Trust is almost always the right structure. It is funded with the parent's assets rather than the beneficiary's. It does not require Medicaid payback at the beneficiary's death. The remainder can pass to other family members or charitable beneficiaries according to the trust's terms. And it can be established as part of the parent's revocable living trust, becoming effective at the parent's death, rather than requiring a separate standalone trust during the parent's lifetime.

The distinction between first-party and third-party trusts — specifically the Medicaid payback requirement — matters enormously for families who want the remaining assets to benefit other family members after the disabled beneficiary passes. A first-party trust, by law, requires that Medicaid be reimbursed for all benefits paid during the beneficiary's lifetime before any remainder passes to heirs. In some cases, the entire trust corpus is consumed by that reimbursement. A third-party trust has no such requirement.

What a Special Needs Trust Can and Cannot Pay For

The trustee of a Special Needs Trust has significant discretion over how trust funds are used, but that discretion is not unlimited. The core principle is that distributions from the trust must supplement government benefits — not replace them. A distribution that pays for something the government program already covers can be counted as income to the beneficiary and reduce their benefits dollar-for-dollar, defeating the trust's purpose.

What an SNT can typically pay for

Supplemental and enhanced care beyond what government programs cover: private therapy sessions, specialized equipment, alternative treatments. Education and vocational training. Recreation, travel, entertainment, and social activities. Technology — computers, tablets, communication devices. Clothing and personal care items beyond what public programs provide. Transportation. Legal and advocacy services. Companion care not covered by Medicaid. A vehicle. Home accessibility modifications. Personal property. Burial expenses.

The common thread is that these are things that improve the beneficiary's quality of life and that government programs either do not cover at all or do not cover adequately.

The trust is filling gaps, not substituting for the base layer of care that SSI and Medicaid provide.

What an SNT generally cannot pay for

Cash directly to the beneficiary — cash counts as income and reduces SSI. Food and shelter paid directly from the trust — these are in-kind income that SSI counts against the benefit. Anything that duplicates what a government program already provides and pays for. The trust cannot be used to funnel assets back to the beneficiary in ways that reconvert trust funds into countable resources.

These restrictions are not arbitrary. They are the rules that preserve the trust's character as a supplement rather than a replacement — the characteristic that keeps it from being counted as the beneficiary's own asset. Violating them, even unintentionally, can jeopardize the beneficiary's benefits retroactively.

> ***Trustee responsibility:*** *The trustee of a Special Needs Trust carries more technical complexity than a standard trust trustee. They need to understand SSI and Medicaid rules, track how distributions affect benefits, and stay current as those rules change. Many families use a professional trustee — or co-trustee a professional with a family member — for exactly this reason.*

Choosing a Trustee for a Special Needs Trust

The trustee of an SNT is making consequential decisions about another person's life — not just financial decisions but decisions about what care, experiences, and quality of life the beneficiary has access to. The qualities required go beyond basic financial competence.

A good SNT trustee understands, or is willing to learn, the complex rules governing SSI and Medicaid distributions. They are committed to the beneficiary's wellbeing, not just to protecting the assets. They communicate well with the beneficiary, their care providers, and other family members. They keep meticulous records — because in the event of a benefits review or a challenge to the trust's administration, documentation is everything. And they are available for the long term, because an SNT may operate for decades.

Individual trustee

A family member who knows and loves the beneficiary, understands their needs, and is willing to invest in learning the relevant rules can be an excellent trustee. The risk is that family members are not always available for the long term, may predecease the beneficiary, may not have the financial or legal sophistication the role requires, or may find that the fiduciary responsibility conflicts with family relationships in ways that become damaging over time.

A sibling or other family member often seems like the obvious choice. Before making that appointment, have an honest conversation about what the role actually entails — the legal fiduciary duty, the documentation requirements, the complexity of SSI and Medicaid distribution rules, and the long-term commitment. The role is not honorary.

Professional or corporate trustee

A trust company, bank trust department, or professional fiduciary brings institutional competence, continuity, and formal accountability. They will not predecease the beneficiary. They have staff who understand the relevant rules. They carry liability insurance. The trade-off is cost — professional trustees typically charge 0.5 to 1.5 percent of trust assets annually — and the potential loss of the personal relationship and advocacy that a loving family member brings.

Co-trustee structure

Many families split the role: a family member serves as co-trustee and advocates for the beneficiary's needs and wishes, while a professional co-trustee handles the financial management, compliance, and documentation. This structure captures the best of both personal knowledge and advocacy from the family, institutional competence and continuity from the professional. It also prevents any single person from having unchecked authority over the trust, which is a protective benefit for the beneficiary as well.

Integrating the SNT into the Parent's Overall Estate Plan

A standalone Special Needs Trust document is one approach. More commonly, and more elegantly, the SNT is incorporated as a sub-trust within the parent's revocable living trust — a specific provision that springs into effect at the parent's death and receives whatever share of the estate the parent designates for the disabled family member.

This integrated approach has several advantages. There is one trust document rather than multiple. The parent maintains control over the SNT's terms during their lifetime without the trust being in effect or having any legal consequence until death. The funding of the SNT happens automatically at the parent's death through the trust's distribution mechanism, without requiring a separate transfer or any action by the family. And the SNT terms can be updated as part of any estate plan review, rather than requiring a separate amendment to a standalone document.

The SNT provision within the parent's trust needs to designate what share or amount is allocated to the disabled beneficiary, who serves as trustee of the SNT sub-trust, what the distribution standards are, and what happens to the remainder when the disabled beneficiary dies. These details require careful drafting by an attorney who specifically understands special needs planning — not just general estate planning.

Life insurance and the SNT

Life insurance is frequently used to fund an SNT, particularly when the parent's estate may not be large enough on its own to provide meaningfully for the disabled family member over a lifetime. The parent takes out a life insurance policy and names the SNT as the beneficiary. At death, the death benefit flows directly into the trust — without probate, without counting as the disabled beneficiary's own asset, and without disrupting any government benefits.

This strategy allows parents with modest estates to provide a meaningful supplement for a disabled family member's lifetime needs without relying entirely on government programs or other family members' ongoing generosity. The insurance benefit is based on what the family estimates the beneficiary will need over their expected lifetime beyond what government programs cover.

Coordinating with siblings and other beneficiaries

When a parent has both a disabled child and non-disabled children, the estate plan needs to address how the SNT allocation relates to what the other children receive. Equal shares in dollar terms may not mean equal benefit in practice — the disabled child's share goes into a trust with restrictions, while the other children's shares are unrestricted. Some parents choose to give the disabled child a larger share to account for anticipated lifetime needs. Others give equal shares and supplement with life insurance specifically directed to the SNT.

There is no universally right answer. What matters is that the decision is deliberate, documented, and explained — ideally to all the children while the parent is alive — so that the non-disabled siblings understand the reasoning rather than experiencing the difference as favoritism.

What Happens If There Is No Special Needs Trust

A parent who dies without an SNT in place, leaving assets directly to a disabled family member who receives SSI or Medicaid, sets the following sequence in motion.

The disabled family member becomes the owner of assets exceeding the program's limit. SSI payments stop immediately. Medicaid coverage is suspended. The family member must spend down the assets to the eligibility threshold before benefits can be restored. During the spend-down period which may last months, depending on the inheritance amount they have no government-funded healthcare coverage, no SSI income support, and may lose their residential placement.

If the family member was in a Medicaid-funded group home or residential program, that placement may be terminated. The waiting list for such placements in most states runs from month to years. The practical consequence is that a sibling or other family member must step in to provide housing and care during the spend-down period care that the parent's estate just made unavailable through an inheritance that was meant to help.

The situation can be partially remedied after the fact through a first-party Special Needs Trust, which can receive the inherited assets and restore Medicaid eligibility — but with the Medicaid payback requirement at death that a third-party SNT avoids. The family effectively pays twice: once in the disruption to the disabled family member's benefits during the gap, and again in Medicaid's reimbursement claim at death that reduces what passes to other heirs. None of this is inevitable. All of it is preventable by including a properly structured SNT in the parent's estate plan before death.

> ***Check all inheritance sources:*** *The SNT needs to be the designated beneficiary not just of the parent's trust but of all assets that might pass to the disabled family member — life insurance policies, retirement accounts with beneficiary designations, and any other asset that might be directed to them by name. A beneficiary designation that names the disabled individual directly, rather than the SNT, triggers the same benefit disruption as a direct inheritance.*

When the Disabled Family Member Is a Sibling, Not a Child

Many parents are also caring for or providing financial support to a disabled adult sibling. The planning dynamics are identical, but the family relationship context is different, and the emotional complexity is worth acknowledging.

The parent who is also supporting a disabled sibling is managing overlapping responsibilities to their own children, to their aging parents, and to the sibling who has been in their care. Estate planning in this context needs to address what happens to the sibling's care and financial support after the parent dies, who steps into the caregiving and advocacy role, and how the estate's resources are allocated among multiple legitimate claims.

A third-party SNT works the same way for a disabled sibling as for a disabled child. The parent names the SNT as the beneficiary of whatever share they want directed to the sibling's care. The trustee ideally someone who knows and is committed to the sibling's wellbeing manages distributions according to the trust's terms. Government benefits are preserved.

The additional consideration for sibling situations is succession planning for the advocacy role. A parent who has been an active advocate for a disabled sibling attending care meetings, managing medications, navigating government programs, fighting for appropriate services needs to designate who takes over that role. The trustee manages the money. Someone else needs to be willing to manage the relationship with service providers, attend meetings, and ensure the sibling's voice is heard. These are different roles that may be filled by the same person or by different people.

> ***Letter of Intent:*** *Many families with disabled dependents prepare a Letter of Intent — a non-binding document that describes the disabled person's daily routines, preferences, relationships, medical history, and what a good life looks like for them. It is addressed to future caregivers and trustees who may not know the person well. The Letter of Intent is not a legal document, but it is one of the most practically useful things a parent can create for a disabled family member's future.*

Finding an Attorney Who Understands Special Needs Planning

Special needs trusts exist at the intersection of estate law, disability law, SSI regulations, Medicaid rules, and tax law. That intersection is complicated, it changes with legislation and regulatory guidance, and it varies by state. A general estate planning attorney who drafts a few SNTs per year is not the same as an attorney who specializes in this area.

Families with a disabled dependent should look specifically for attorneys who identify themselves as special needs planning attorneys, who belong to the Special Needs Alliance or the Academy of Special Needs Planners, and who can demonstrate regular, ongoing experience with SNT drafting and administration. The quality of the drafting matters enormously an SNT that is structured incorrectly or that fails to include the right language can fail to protect benefits even when the intent was correct.

The Special Needs Alliance maintains a searchable directory of member attorneys at specialneedsalliance.org. These attorneys have signed on to specific standards of practice in the special needs planning area and are a reliable starting point for families who need to find qualified counsel.

If your parent has a disabled dependent and their current estate plan does not include a properly drafted Special Needs Trust, correcting that gap is the highest-priority estate planning action in this book. Everything else in the plan can be refined later. An SNT that does not exist cannot be refined and a direct inheritance to a benefits-dependent family member cannot be undone once it has occurred.

The Most Important Thing Your Parent Can Leave

A Special Needs Trust is not just a financial instrument. It is a parent's way of staying present in a disabled family member's life after they are gone — of ensuring that their love, their resources, and their intentions continue to shape that person's quality of life for decades.

Parents of disabled children carry a particular weight: the knowledge that their child's wellbeing is tied to their own longevity and capacity in ways that other parents' relationships are not. Planning around that reality — honestly, specifically, and with the right legal tools — is one of the most profound acts of care a parent can undertake.

It is also, practically, straightforward once the right attorney is engaged. The legal tools exist. The rules are knowable. The drafting is specific but not unknowable. What the planning requires is the decision to do it, and to do it now, while there is still time to get it right. Part Five of this book moves into the mechanics of setting it all up — how to choose and structure the right trust, how to fund it, whether you need an attorney and how to find a good one, and the master checklist that takes the family from first conversation to signed documents. Chapter 15 starts with the living trust setup process itself.

PART FIVE: SETTING IT ALL UP

The Step-by-Step Family Organizer Process

CHAPTER 15

How to Set Up the Living Trust: A Plain-Language Walkthrough

Setting up a living trust is not complicated. It requires the right attorney, the right decisions about trustees and beneficiaries, and critically the follow-through to fund it. This chapter walks through each step, so you know exactly what to expect and what questions to ask.

What the Setup Process Actually Looks Like

Families who have never been through estate planning often imagine the process is more complicated, more formal, or more expensive than it is. The reality is that setting up a living trust typically involves three to four meetings with an attorney over four to eight weeks, a signing ceremony once the documents are complete, and then the funding process that transfers assets into the trust.

That is the whole thing. There is no court involvement, no public filing, no judge. The trust is a private contract between your parent and their trustee — which is initially themselves. The attorney drafts it, your parent reviews it, they sign it in front of a notary and witnesses, and it exists. What makes it effective is the funding that follows.

Most families find the process less daunting than expected once they understand the steps. The anxiety tends to be about the conversation that precedes the attorney engagement, not about the legal process itself. If you have read this far, you have already done the harder work.

Step One: Choose the Right Type of Trust

Not all living trusts are identical. The basic structure is consistent — a revocable trust that the grantor controls during their lifetime, with a successor trustee who takes over at incapacity or death — but the specific terms and provisions vary based on the family's situation. Before engaging an attorney, it helps to understand what decisions need to be made.

Revocable vs. irrevocable

For most aging parents, the appropriate choice is a revocable living trust one they can modify, fund, or terminate at any point during their lifetime. The trade-off for that flexibility is that a revocable trust does not provide asset protection from creditors or Medicaid during the grantor's lifetime. Assets in a revocable trust are still considered the grantor's own assets for most legal purposes.

An irrevocable trust, like the Medicaid Asset Protection Trust covered in Chapter 8, gives up that flexibility in exchange for real asset protection. Once assets are in an irrevocable trust, the grantor cannot take them back. Irrevocable trusts serve specific planning purposes and are not appropriate as the primary estate planning vehicle for most families.

Single vs. joint trust

Married couples can each have their own individual trust, or they can establish a joint revocable living trust that holds both spouses' assets. Joint trusts are simpler to administer during the couple's lifetime one document, one set of records, one funding process. They work best for couples with relatively equal assets, shared beneficiary goals, and no blended family complexity.

Individual trust for each spouse provide more flexibility when spouses have significantly different assets, different beneficiary intentions, or a blended family situation where each spouse wants to control the disposition of their own assets independently. They also simplify administration at the first death, because the deceased spouse's trust is already separate and does not need to be divided.

For blended families, as Chapter 13 covered, individual trusts with specific provisions for the surviving spouse — such as a QTIP sub-trust — are almost always the better structure than a joint trust that treats everything as shared.

Standard revocable trust vs. trust with sub-trusts

A simple revocable living trust distributes assets to named beneficiaries at the grantor's death, much like a will but without probate. This is appropriate when beneficiaries are adults with no special circumstances.

A trust with sub-trusts holds assets in trust for beneficiaries under specific conditions rather than distributing them outright. Sub-trusts are used when a beneficiary is a minor (holding assets until they reach a specified age), has a substance abuse or financial management issue (distributing only under certain conditions), has special needs (as Chapter 14 covered), or when the estate is large enough that ongoing management and tax planning justify keeping assets in trust rather than distributing them immediately.

Most middle-class estates use a straightforward revocable trust with outright distribution at death. Sub-trusts add complexity and are appropriate when the specific circumstances justify it.

Step Two: Choose the Trustees

The trustee decisions are the most consequential decisions in the entire trust setup process. They determine who has legal authority over the assets, who makes distribution decisions, and who your parents trust with the financial future they have spent a lifetime building.

Three trustee roles need to be filled.

Initial trustee

Your parents serve as their own initial trustee. This is standard and expected. During their lifetime and while they have capacity, they manage the trust assets exactly as they managed their own assets before. Nothing about their day-to-day financial life changes.

Successor trustee

The successor trustee is the person or institution that takes over when your parent can no longer serve at death or incapacity. This is the appointment that matters most.

The successor trustee needs to be honest, organized, financially capable, available when needed, and able to deal with financial institutions, attorneys, and potentially contentious family members without becoming overwhelmed or compromised. Being a loving family member is a starting point, not a sufficient qualification on its own.

They also need to be willing to serve. Have the conversation explicitly. Do not assume that because someone is the obvious choice, they are prepared for what the role involves. A successor trustee who discovers the scope of the responsibility at the worst possible moment

— in the immediate aftermath of a parent's death — is a problem that a candid conversation beforehand would have prevented.

Backup successor trustee

Name at least one backup. The first choice may be unable or unwilling to serve when the time comes. A trust with no functioning successor trustee requires court intervention to appoint one, which defeats the purpose of having a trust in the first place.

	Family Member Trustee	Professional / Corporate Trustee
Cost	Usually none, or minimal	0.5–1.5% of assets annually
Knowledge of the family	High — knows the beneficiaries personally	Low — manages from a distance
Financial / legal expertise	Varies widely — may need support	High — institutional competence
Longevity	May predecease beneficiaries or become incapacitated	Institutional continuity — no succession problem
Family conflict risk	Higher — may be perceived as favoring one side	Lower — neutral third party
Accountability	Legal fiduciary duty but limited practical oversight unless challenged	Regulated, bonded, subject to regular audits
Best for	Smaller estates, close families, trusted and capable individual	Larger estates, complex situations, high-conflict families, long-duration trusts

The co-trustee structure — combining a family member and a professional trustee is worth considering when the estate is large enough to justify the cost, when family dynamics suggest a neutral party would reduce conflict, or when the family member trustee lacks the financial expertise, the role requires but has irreplaceable personal knowledge of the beneficiaries.

> ***Practical advice:*** *Before naming someone as successor trustee, sit down with them and walk through what the role actually involves: inventorying assets, contacting financial institutions, filing a final tax return, potentially selling the family home, distributing assets, and dealing with any creditor claims or family disputes. Make sure they understand what they're agreeing to.*

Step Three: Name the Beneficiaries

The beneficiaries are the people who receive the trust assets at your parent's death. Naming them correctly requires clarity about who receives what, in what proportions, and under what conditions.

Primary beneficiaries

Primary beneficiaries receive assets at your parent's death. They should be named specifically — by full legal name, relationship, and date of birth if helpful — rather than by description. "My children" sounds clear but creates questions if a child predeceases the grantor, if there are stepchildren, or if a child is born after the trust is created.

Naming each beneficiary by name eliminates ambiguity.

The trust also needs to specify proportions. Equal shares among children are common but not universal. A trust that says "equal shares to my three children" is clear. A trust that says "the majority of my estate to my daughter who has been my caregiver, with a smaller portion to my son" needs to specify percentages, not adjectives.

Contingent beneficiaries

A contingent beneficiary receives assets if a primary beneficiary predeceases the grantor. Without a contingent designation, a deceased primary beneficiary's share typically falls back into the trust and is redistributed among surviving primary beneficiaries — which may or may not be what your parent intends. If your parent wants a deceased child's share to pass to that child's own children (per stirpes distribution), that needs to be specified explicitly.

Distribution age for minor beneficiaries

If any beneficiary is or might be a minor at the time of distribution, the trust needs to specify at what age they receive their inheritance outright. Distributing $200,000 to an 18-year-old is legal. Whether it is wise is a different question. Many trusts stagger distributions — one-third at 25, one-third at 30, the balance at 35 — to give beneficiaries time to develop the judgment that a large inheritance requires.

Specific bequests

If your parents want specific items of personal property — jewelry, furniture, vehicles, collections, family heirlooms — to go to specific people, those wishes can be addressed either in the trust itself or in a separate personal property memorandum that is referenced in the trust. The memorandum approach allows your parents to update specific bequests without amending the trust document, which is more flexible and usually more practical.

Step Four: Sign the Documents Correctly

A trust document that is not properly executed is not a valid trust. Execution requirements vary by state but typically include your parents' signature before a notary and, in some states, one or two witnesses. The attorney managing the signing will ensure the formalities are met — this is not something to improvise or do informally.

The signing ceremony is also the moment when the attorney confirms that your parent has the legal capacity to execute the documents, understands what they are signing, and is acting freely without undue influence. As Chapter 11 covered, this assessment matters and should be taken seriously. An attorney who waves clients through a signing without assessing capacity is not doing their job.

At the signing, your parents should also execute the pour-over will, the durable power of attorney, the healthcare directive, and the HIPAA authorization. All five documents should be completed together, not piecemeal over time, unless there is a specific reason to separate them.

> ***Keep originals safe:*** *The original signed trust document should be stored somewhere secure and accessible — a fireproof home safe, a safe deposit box, or with the attorney. A copy should be provided to the successor trustee so they know where it is and what it contains. A trust that cannot be located when needed is functionally no different from a trust that was never created.*

Step Five: Fund the Trust

This is the step that most families underestimate and that most estate planning failures trace back to. A signed, executed living trust that has not been funded provides no probate protection. Assets that remain titled in your parent's individual name at death go through probate — regardless of what the trust says.

Funding the trust means transferring ownership of assets from your parent's individual name into the trust's name. The trust's name is typically something like "John Smith, Trustee of the John Smith Revocable Living Trust dated January 15, 2025." That is the legal name that appears on deeds, account titles, and ownership documents for assets held in the trust.

Asset Type	How to Fund into Trust	Who Does the Work	Goes in Trust?
Primary residence	New deed prepared and recorded with county	Attorney or title company	Yes
Other real estate	New deeds prepared and recorded in each county	Attorney (each state where property located)	Yes
Bank accounts (checking, savings)	Visit bank; retitle account to trust or add POD	Your parent, in person at the bank	Yes
Brokerage / investment accounts	Contact firm to retitle account or add TOD beneficiary	Your parent, by phone/mail/online with the institution	Yes
IRA / 401(k) / retirement accounts	Do NOT retitle — update beneficiary designation instead	Your parent, with the plan administrator	No*
Life insurance	Update beneficiary designation to trust (or named individuals)	Your parent, with the insurance company	No*
Tangible personal property	Assignment document or schedule attached to trust	Attorney or self with attorney review	Yes

Vehicles (cars, boats)	Usually NOT transferred — use TOD title where available, or leave out	DMV or state motor vehicles office	Usually no

Retirement accounts and life insurance should NOT be retitled into a revocable living trust. Doing so can trigger immediate taxation of the entire retirement account balance. Instead, these assets pass by beneficiary designation. The trust can be named as the beneficiary if specific planning goals require it, but this needs careful attorney guidance on the tax implications.

> ***The most common funding gap:*** *Real estate is the asset families most often think is in the trust when it isn't. A deed must be physically prepared, signed, and recorded with the county recorder's office to transfer real property into the trust. The intent to transfer it is not enough. Pull the current deed from the county recorder's website — most counties make this searchable for free — and verify that the trust is listed as the owner. If it isn't, that deed needs to be fixed now.*

The Funding Walkthrough: Asset by Asset

Real estate

The attorney prepares a new deed transferring the property from your parent's name to the trust. The document is signed by your parents and recorded with the county recorder's office in the county where the property is located. If your parent owns real estate in multiple states, each state requires its own deed prepared in compliance with that state's recording requirements.

Recording fees are typically modest — $15 to $100 depending on the county — and transfer taxes are usually exempt for transfers to a revocable living trust. Check your state's rules. Most states also have a provision that prevents the transfer from triggering the mortgage's due-on-sale clause when the transfer is to a revocable trust where the borrower is also the trustee.

Property tax exemptions, including homestead exemptions, are generally not affected by a transfer to a revocable living trust, but confirm this with the county assessor's office in your parent's jurisdiction before completing the transfer.

Bank and investment accounts

Contact the financial institution directly. Some banks will retitle an existing account to the trust; others require closing the existing account and opening a new one in the trust's name. Either way, the end result is an account owned by the trust rather than by your parent individually.

Bring a copy of the trust document or a certification of trust certificate. the attorney can prepare that summarizes the trust's key provisions without disclosing the full distribution terms to the bank. Most institutions will accept a certification rather than requiring the full trust document.

For accounts where your parent prefers not to retitle into the trust perhaps a checking account they use for daily expenses and find the trust name cumbersome adding a payable-on-death beneficiary to the account is an acceptable alternative that still allows the account to transfer without probate.

Business interests

Transferring a membership interest in an LLC or a partnership interest into a trust requires reviewing the operating agreement or partnership agreement first. Many operating agreements restrict transfers of membership interests or require consent from other members. If the operating agreement allows transfer to a revocable living trust, the transfer is accomplished through an assignment document. If it does not, the operating agreement may need to be amended, or the interest may need to be structured differently.

This is one area where DIY funding attempts most commonly go wrong. Get attorney guidance before transferring any business interest into a trust.

Personal property

Vehicles, jewelry, art, collectibles, furniture, and other tangible personal property can be transferred to the trust through a general assignment document a simple written statement that the owner assigns all tangible personal property to the trust. The attorney can prepare this as part of the trust package.

Vehicles are an exception in most states. Retitling a vehicle into a trust name requires a new title through the state's motor vehicle department, which is administratively cumbersome and often not worth the effort for most vehicles. Many states now allow transfer-on-death designations for vehicle titles, which accomplish the same probate- avoidance goal more simply. Check your parents' state's rules.

After Funding: Keeping the Trust Current

The trust is not a one-time project. Every time your parent acquires a new asset opens a new bank account, buys a new property, receives a significant gift that asset needs to be transferred into the trust or positioned to transfer outside of probate through another mechanism. A trust that was fully funded five years ago and hasn't been reviewed since may have gaps that undo part of its protection.

The simplest way to maintain the trust's completeness is to make it a habit: any time your parents take a significant financial action, ask whether the new asset is going into the trust. Open a new CD? Name the trust as owner. Receive an inheritance from another family member? Transfer it into the trust. Buying a vacation property? Have a deed prepared to put it in the trust immediately.

The asset inventory built in Chapter 7 is the tool for tracking this. An updated inventory reviewed annually or after any significant financial change should match the assets held in the trust. Any discrepancy is a gap that needs to be closed.

> ***Quick verification:*** *Pull a current statement for every major account and check whose name appears as account owner. It should read "[Parent's name], Trustee of the [Trust name]" or similar. If it reads just your parent's name, the account has not been funded into the trust.*

What to Expect from the Attorney Engagement

A typical living trust engagement with an elder law or estate planning attorney proceeds in a predictable sequence. Understanding the sequence helps families know what to prepare, what to expect at each stage, and how to evaluate whether the process is proceeding appropriately.

Initial consultation

The first meeting is information-gathering. The attorney will ask about your parent's family situation, assets, goals, and any complicating factors — blended family dynamics, disabled dependents, business interests, Medicaid concerns. This is not the time to hold anything back. The attorney can only draft a plan that addresses your parent's actual situation if they know what it is.

Come to this meeting with the asset inventory from Chapter 7, a clear sense of who your parents want as successor trustee, and a list of beneficiaries and their relationships. The more prepared your parents are, the more efficient this meeting will proceed.

Draft review

The attorney prepares draft documents — typically within one to three weeks for a standard engagement — and sends them for review. This is the moment when your parents read through what the attorney has drafted and confirms it reflects their actual wishes. Errors in beneficiary names, incorrect asset descriptions, trustee appointments that don't match what was discussed — all of this is caught here, before signing. Take this review seriously. A trust document is a binding legal instrument. Assuming the attorney got everything right without reading it is how mistakes get signed into effect.

Signing

The signing meeting is typically brief — an hour or less for a standard package. The attorney walks through each document, confirms your parent understands what they are signing, and supervises the execution formalities. The trust and pour-over will require notarization; other documents may have additional requirements depending on the state.

Funding

Some attorneys handle the funding process as part of their engagement fee. Others prepare the deed for the primary residence and leave remaining accounts for the client to handle. Clarify this before engagement, not after signing. If the attorney is not handling funding, ask for a specific funding checklist for each asset type so the process is clear.

Chapter 16 covers how to find and vet the right attorney, what fair fees look like, and when a DIY approach is and is not appropriate.

The Difference Between a Trust That Exists and a Trust That Works

More families have a living trust document sitting in a drawer than most people realize. The document exists. The attorney was paid. The signing happened. And then the funding didn't. The house is still in your parents' name. The bank accounts were never retitled. The trust is a piece of paper with no practical effect.

A trust that works one that keeps assets out of probate, actually enables the successor trustee to step in without court involvement, actually transfers the home to the right people without delay — is a funded trust. The document and the funding together. Neither one without the other.

If your parents already have a trust, the most important question is whether it is funded. Pull the deed. Check the account titles. Review the asset inventory against what the trust owns. If there are gaps, they can be fixed now — and fixing them now is exactly the kind of practical action that this book exists to enable.

Chapter 16 answers the question families ask next: do we actually need an attorney for all of this, and if so, how do we find a good one without overpaying?

CHAPTER 16

Do You Need a Lawyer? A Realistic Guide

The honest answer is for most families with aging parents, yes. But not for every situation, not at any price, and not from just any attorney. This chapter gives you a clear framework for when DIY is reasonable, how to find qualified counsel, what fair fees look like, and how to spot the red flags that signal you're in the wrong office.

The Honest Case for Professional Help

There is a version of this question that sounds like: "Can I avoid paying an attorney?" That is a reasonable thing to wonder. Attorney fees are real, they are not trivial, and the internet is full of tools that promise to deliver estate planning documents for a fraction of the cost.

Here is the accurate framing: you are not paying an attorney to fill out forms. You are paying for the legal judgment to know which forms are right for your parent's specific situation, how to draft them so they accomplish what your parent intends, how to spot the issues your parent didn't know to raise, and how to ensure the documents will hold up under the scrutiny that sometimes follows a death or incapacity.

A form filled out correctly produces a valid document. A form filled out incorrectly — with the wrong trust type, the wrong beneficiary language, the wrong trustee provisions for the family's dynamics — produces a valid document that does the wrong thing. The legal fees that follow discovering that error after your parent's death routinely exceed what a competent attorney would have charged to get it right the first time.

That said, not every estate requires a full attorney engagement. There are situations where simpler approaches are genuinely adequate, and being honest about those situations is part of giving families accurate guidance rather than blanket recommendations driven by anything other than their actual needs.

> *An online estate planning tool is like a map. It can get you where you're going if the terrain is straightforward. When the terrain gets complicated — a blended family, a disabled dependent, a Medicaid concern, cognitive decline — you need someone who can read the land, not just the map.*

When DIY Is Reasonable and When It Isn't

The table below is a genuine decision framework, not a soft push toward hiring an attorney regardless of circumstances. Use it honestly.

DIY May Be Reasonable When…	An Attorney Is Needed When…
The estate consists of a few accounts with named beneficiaries and little else	Real estate is owned, especially in multiple states
All assets already pass by beneficiary designation or joint ownership	There is any blended family, second marriage, or stepparent dynamic
The estate falls below the state's small estate threshold	A family member has special needs or receives government benefits
Family relationships are uncomplicated and all parties agree	There is any cognitive decline concern that could affect document validity
The goal is only to update beneficiary designations on existing accounts	Medicaid planning is a concern now or within the next five years
A very simple will is the appropriate document — not a trust	A business interest is part of the estate
The person has basic financial literacy and is willing to research carefully	Any prior disputes, estrangements, or litigation involving the family

The right column is not a list of edge cases. Most families with aging parents will find at least one item on that list that applies to their situation. Real estate alone — which covers the majority of aging parents who own a home — puts an attorney in the picture for the deed transfer if nothing else.

The DIY column is not a trap either. A parent whose estate consists of a few bank accounts with named beneficiaries, no real estate, no blended family complications, and whose primary goal is a simple will to direct personal property — that family may genuinely be well served by an online tool or a basic attorney consultation rather than a full trust engagement.

The question to answer honestly is: which column describes my parent's actual situation? Not the simplified version, not the one that makes the next step feel easier, but the actual situation including all the complications.

> ***The false economy:*** *Families who use an online tool for a situation that belongs in the right column sometimes discover the problem at the worst possible time. A trust drafted without understanding the blended family dynamics, an SNT omitted because the online tool didn't surface the issue, a deed not transferred because the tool didn't include the funding step — these are not hypothetical failures. They are the kinds of failures that generate the legal fees that an attorney engagement would have prevented.*

General Attorney vs. Elder Law Attorney: The Difference Matters

Not all estate planning attorneys are the same. The distinction between a general estate planning attorney and an elder law attorney is not about credentials or quality in the abstract — it is about specialization, and it matters for families with aging parents.

General estate planning attorney

A general estate planning attorney drafts wills, trusts, powers of attorney, and healthcare directives. They understand the mechanics of estate administration, probate avoidance, and basic tax planning. For a straightforward estate plan — a trust, a will, the supporting documents, and basic beneficiary planning — a general estate planning attorney is adequate and often less expensive than an elder law specialist.

Elder law attorney

An elder law attorney has additional specialized knowledge in the areas most relevant to aging families: Medicaid planning, long-term care planning, Special Needs Trust drafting and administration, cognitive decline and capacity issues, elder financial exploitation, and the intersection of estate planning with government benefit programs. The National Elder Law

Foundation (NELF) offers a Certified Elder Law Attorney (CELA) designation that signals demonstrated competency in this specialty.

For families where any of the following apply — Medicaid planning is a concern, a family member has a disability, cognitive decline has begun, a MAPT or SNT is needed, or the estate is approaching the Medicaid eligibility threshold — an elder law attorney is not a premium option. It is the baseline appropriate choice.

The fee difference between a general estate planning attorney and an elder law attorney for a standard trust package is typically modest. The difference in expertise for the specific situations where elder law knowledge matters is not modest at all.

> ***How to verify:*** *The National Academy of Elder Law Attorneys (NAELA) and the Special Needs Alliance both maintain searchable online directories of member attorneys by state. CELA designation through NELF requires passing a comprehensive examination and demonstrating substantial elder law experience. These are reliable starting points for finding qualified counsel.*

What a Qualified Attorney Should Cost

Fee transparency is one area where the estate planning industry has historically done families a disservice. The range of fees charged for identical services is wide, the justifications offered for higher fees are often opaque, and families have no reliable benchmark to evaluate whether what they're being quoted is reasonable.

The table below provides realistic fee ranges based on current market rates across most U.S. regions. Costs in major metropolitan areas run toward the higher end; smaller markets run lower. These are ranges, not guarantees, and complexity in any individual situation can push costs higher. But they give you a baseline to evaluate what you're being quoted.

Service	Reasonable Fee Range	Red Flag If...
Basic will (individual)	$300–$800	Over $1,500 for a simple will with no complicating factors

Revocable living trust (individual, includes pour-over will)	$1,500–$3,500	Under $800 (likely template, minimal customization) or over $5,000 without clear justification
Full estate plan package (trust, will, DPOA, healthcare directive, HIPAA)	$2,500–$5,000	Quoted as hourly without a clear estimate; no package pricing available
Complex trust (blended family, SNT, MAPT, business interests)	$4,000–$10,000+	Complexity is used to justify fees without explanation of what specifically adds cost
Real estate deed transfer to trust	$200–$600 per property	Over $1,000 for a straightforward residential deed in a single county
Trust amendment	$300–$800	Flat fee equal to or exceeding original trust cost for a simple change

Flat fee pricing is generally preferable to hourly billing for estate planning work. With a flat fee, you know exactly what you're paying before the work begins, and the attorney has an incentive to work efficiently rather than to generate billable hours. Most estate planning attorneys offer flat fee packages for standard engagements.

Hourly billing is appropriate for complex matters where the scope cannot be defined in advance — contested capacity situations, disputes, or complex Medicaid planning that may require negotiation with state agencies. For a standard trust package, hourly billing without a clear estimate and billing cap is a structure that benefits the attorney more than the client.

How to Find a Good Attorney Without Wasting Time

The search for an estate planning attorney is more manageable than most families expect, particularly now that online directories and state bar resources make it possible to identify candidates quickly. The process has three stages: generating candidates, vetting them, and making the selection.

Generating candidates

Start with the directories. The National Academy of Elder Law Attorneys (naela.org), the Special Needs Alliance (specialneedsalliance.org), and your state bar association's referral service all provide searchable lists of attorneys by location and specialty. A CELA designation or NAELA membership is not a guarantee of quality, but it is a signal that the attorney has invested in the specialty rather than treating estate planning as an occasional side service.

Personal referrals are valuable when they come from people with direct experience. A family member or friend who worked with an attorney recently and had a good experience is a meaningful recommendation. A referral from someone who used an attorney once fifteen years ago for something unrelated is less so.

Financial advisors, CPAs, and geriatric care managers who work regularly with aging families often have working relationships with elder law attorneys they've seen perform well across multiple client situations. These referrals tend to be better-informed than random recommendations.

Vetting candidates

Initial consultations are standard practice and usually free or low-cost. Schedule consultations with two or three candidates before deciding. This is not disrespectful to the attorneys it is appropriate due diligence, and any attorney who discourages a second opinion is giving you useful information.

State bar discipline records are publicly searchable in most states. Check whether your candidates have any disciplinary history. A single minor complaint from years ago may be unremarkable. A pattern of complaints, or any finding involving client funds, is disqualifying.

What to evaluate in the consultation

Listen to whether the attorney asks more questions than they answer in the initial meeting. A good estate planning attorney needs to understand your parent's complete situation before recommending a plan. An attorney who leads with recommendations before understanding the situation is not working from adequate information.

Assess whether they explain things in plain language or retreat into jargon when pressed. The documents they will draft are complex. Their job includes making that complexity comprehensible. An attorney who cannot explain their own recommendations clearly is a problem.

Notice whether they identify issues you hadn't considered. A specialist who has seen hundreds of similar situations will typically surface concerns that a family didn't know how to raise. An attorney who simply takes your instructions without pushing back or expanding the conversation may be efficient, but they may also be missing something.

Question to Ask	What a Good Answer Sounds Like
What percentage of your practice is estate planning or elder law?	A majority, or a clearly defined specialty area. Wariness if estate planning is occasional work alongside unrelated practice areas.
Do you handle the funding process, or is that left to us?	Clear answer either way. If not included, ask for a written funding checklist for every asset type.
How do you assess whether a client has the legal capacity to sign?	A specific process — private meeting with the client, specific questions, physician letter if needed. Not "we just have them sign."
What is your fee structure — flat fee or hourly?	Flat fee with a clear scope of what is included. Hourly is not automatically wrong but requires a clear estimate and billing transparency.
How will you handle this if our situation involves [specific complexity]?	A specific, informed answer that demonstrates they've handled similar situations, not a generic reassurance.
How long will the process take from first meeting to signed documents?	A realistic timeline — typically four to eight weeks for a standard engagement. Significantly longer without explanation

	suggests capacity issues at the firm.
What happens if we need to update the plan in a few years?	A clear process for amendments and an indication of typical costs. An attorney who discourages future updates is not thinking about your parent's long-term interests.

Red Flags That Signal You're in the Wrong Office

Some of these are obvious. Some are subtle. All of them are worth knowing before you sign an engagement letter.

High-pressure sales tactics

An attorney who creates urgency around purchasing additional services, who implies that declining a recommendation puts your parent at serious risk, or who makes you feel that the standard package is inadequate without a clear explanation of why is not practicing law — they are selling. Estate planning attorneys who lead with service upselling rather than honest assessment of what the client actually needs are a problem.

One-size-fits-all recommendations

If an attorney recommends the same trust structure for every client regardless of family situation, asset composition, or stated goals, they are working from a template rather than from professional judgment. A recommendation that does not engage with the specific complexities of your parent's situation — the blended family, the Medicaid concern, the sibling dynamics, the cognitive decline — is not a tailored plan. It is a form with a name on it.

Resistance to questions

An attorney who becomes defensive when asked to explain their recommendations, who dismisses concerns with reassurance rather than explanations, or who discourages a second opinion is not behaving professionally. Questions about fee structure, scope of services, and the reasoning behind specific recommendations are normal and appropriate. Any attorney who makes a client feel that asking those questions is a sign of distrust is not the right attorney.

Unrealistically low fees

A full trust package offered for significantly below the market range is almost always a template document with minimal customization, minimal attorney involvement, and minimal attention to the family's specific circumstances. The document may be technically valid while being entirely inappropriate for the situation. An unusually low quote warrants the question: what exactly is included, and how much time will you personally spend on our plan?

No discussion of funding

An attorney who drafts a trust but never mentions the funding process — who does not address how assets will be transferred into the trust, whether they handle the deed transfer, or what the family needs to do on their own — is setting the family up for the most common estate planning failure. Funding is not optional paperwork. It is the step that makes the trust work. Any attorney who treats it as the client's problem to figure out independently is not providing complete service.

Pressuring a parent with cognitive concerns

An attorney who proceeds with a signing without assessing capacity, who allows a cognitively impaired client to be coached through document execution by a family member in the room, or who does not meet privately with the client before signing is not doing their job and is potentially facilitating undue influence. If you observe this behavior in an attorney working with your parents, it is a serious problem that warrants reporting to the state bar.

> ***Trust your instincts:*** *If an attorney makes your parent feel rushed, confused, or pressured, that is information. Legal documents signed under those conditions are more vulnerable to challenge and may not reflect your parents' actual wishes. The right attorney makes the process feel manageable, not overwhelming.*

Online Tools: What They Can and Cannot Do Safely

Online estate planning platforms have improved significantly and are a legitimate option for genuinely simple situations. Understanding their actual capabilities and limitations helps families use them appropriately rather than either dismissing them entirely or over-relying on them.

What online tools do well

Generating basic will documents for straightforward situations. Providing DPOA and healthcare directive templates that meet the formal requirements of most states.

Organizing beneficiary designation updates across multiple accounts through guided workflows. Educating users about estate planning concepts in accessible language. Providing a starting point for families who need to understand what documents they need before engaging an attorney.

What online tools cannot do

Assess your parents' specific situation and identify issues the family hasn't recognized. Evaluate legal capacity or notice signs of undue influence. Draft trust provisions tailored to blended family dynamics, special needs dependents, or Medicaid planning requirements. Prepare and record real estate deeds that comply with county-specific recording requirements. Provide legal advice when something goes wrong.

Online tools produce documents based on information the user provides. They cannot ask the follow-up question that surfaces the complicated factor the user didn't know to mention. A family that completes an online trust without realizing their parent has an LLC, a property in another state, or a family member with disabilities has produced a document that is technically valid and functionally incomplete.

The appropriate use

Online tools are appropriate for updating beneficiary designations, for generating a basic will in a genuinely simple estate, and for educating a family before they engage an attorney. They are a complement to professional advice for simple situations, not a replacement for professional advice in complex ones.

If a family completes an online tool and then has it reviewed by an elder law attorney before signing, they have likely gotten good value from both resources. If they complete it and treat it as done without any professional review, they may have created a false sense of security that is only discovered when the document is tested.

> ***A useful middle path:*** *Some families complete an online planning tool, use it to organize their thinking and gather the information an attorney will need, and then bring that to a one-hour consultation with an attorney to review what they've produced and identify any gaps. That approach captures the efficiency of the online tool while ensuring a professional eye has reviewed the plan.*

The Right Help at the Right Cost

The goal of this chapter is not to convince every family that they need the most expensive attorney available. The goal is to help families make an informed decision about what kind of help their parent's specific situation actually requires — and then to find that help at a fair price from a qualified person.

For most families with aging parents who own real estate, the answer is a qualified estate planning or elder law attorney for the core documents and deed transfer, with online tools as a complement for simpler tasks like updating beneficiary designations. For families with blended family dynamics, Medicaid concerns, cognitive decline, or a disabled dependent, the answer is an elder law specialist who knows this territory specifically.

The fee for that engagement is real. It is also, for most families, a fraction of what probate costs, what a conservatorship costs, or what a poorly structured plan costs to repair. The investment in getting it right is not a luxury. For aging families, it is one of the most cost-effective financial decisions available.

Chapter 17 brings everything together in a master checklist — the complete step-by- step action plan from first conversation to signed documents and funded trust.

CHAPTER 17

The Family Organizer's Master Checklist

Sixteen chapters of knowledge distilled into a single action sequence. This chapter is designed to be used, not just read — printed out, worked through, checked off, and kept with the estate documents as a record of what has been done and what still needs doing.

How to Use This Chapter

This checklist is organized in four phases based on where most families start: before a single conversation has happened, through the attorney engagement, through the funding process, and into ongoing maintenance. Not every family starts at the beginning
some have a partial plan already in place, some are responding to an emerging health situation, some have been through the conversation and just need to know what comes next. Start wherever your parents' situation puts you. If documents are already signed, skip to the funding phase and verify what was and wasn't completed. If conversations have already happened, skip to the attorney engagement phase. If you are at the very beginning, work through it from Phase One.

Every item on this list traces back to a chapter in this book. Where a decision is complex or context-dependent, the relevant chapter is referenced so you can return to the full explanation. The checklist tells you what to do. The chapters tell you why and how.

> ***Print this chapter:*** *This checklist is most useful as a physical document that gets worked through over time, marked up, and kept with the estate papers. Print it, use it as a working document, and update it as items are completed. A digital checklist nobody looks at is worth less than a marked-up paper one that lives in the folder with the trust.*

PHASE ONE

Before the Attorney: Conversations, Inventory, and Decisions

Complete before scheduling the attorney consultation

The Conversation

- ☐ Have the initial estate planning conversation with your parents or confirm it has already happened (Chapter 2)
- ☐ Identify which siblings or family members need to be involved in planning discussions (Chapter 3)
- ☐ If applicable: hold a family meeting to align roles, responsibilities, and expectations (Chapter 3)
- ☐ Discuss your parents' wishes for healthcare decisions, end-of-life care, and specific medical interventions (Chapter 5)
- ☐ If cognitive concerns exist assess urgency and prioritize document execution timeline (Chapter 11.

The Inventory

- ☐ Complete a full asset inventory covering all eight categories (Chapter 7)
- ☐ Real estate: address, titling, mortgage status, estimated value, location of deed for each property
- ☐ Bank and credit union accounts: institution, account numbers, titling, POD designation for each
- ☐ Investment and brokerage accounts: institution, account numbers, titling, TOD designation, cost basis
- ☐ Retirement accounts: type, institution, account numbers, current beneficiary designations for each
- ☐ Life insurance policies: company, policy number, death benefit, beneficiary designations for each
- ☐ Digital assets: financial accounts, email, social media, photo storage, cryptocurrency, subscriptions

- ☐ Business interests: entity type, ownership percentage, location of operating agreement
- ☐ Debts and obligations: mortgages, loans, co-signed debt, ongoing financial obligations
- ☐ Safe deposit box: location, key location, who else has access
- ☐ Review last 3–5 years of tax returns to cross-check inventory completeness
- ☐ Search state unclaimed property database for any dormant or forgotten accounts

Beneficiary Designations — Preliminary Review

- ☐ Pull current beneficiary designations for all retirement accounts (Chapter 10)
- ☐ Pull current beneficiary designations for all life insurance policies (Chapter 10)
- ☐ Pull current POD/TOD designations for bank and brokerage accounts (Chapter 10)
- ☐ Flag any designations naming: a deceased person, an ex-spouse, a minor child directly, or "estate" as beneficiary
- ☐ Flag any accounts with no contingent beneficiary named

Key Decisions to Make Before the Attorney Meeting

- ☐ Identify who should serve as successor trustee (and backup) have the conversation with them explicitly (Chapter 15)
- ☐ Identify who should serve as DPOA agent (and backup) have the conversation with them explicitly (Chapter 5)
- ☐ Identify who should serve as healthcare agent (and backup) have the conversation with them explicitly (Chapter 5)
- ☐ Identify primary and contingent beneficiaries with full legal names
- ☐ If minor beneficiaries: decide at what age(s) they should receive distributions (Chapter 15)
- ☐ If blended family: discuss and agree on structure with spouse before the attorney meeting (Chapter 13)
- ☐ If special needs dependent: confirm SNT is needed and identify trustee candidate (Chapter 14)

□ If Medicaid is a concern: research five-year lookback timing relative to parent's health situation (Chapter 8, 9)

PHASE TWO

The Attorney Engagement

From first consultation through signed documents

Finding the Right Attorney

□ Determine whether a general estate planning attorney or elder law specialist is needed (Chapter 16)

□ Generate 2–3 candidates using NAELA directory, state bar referral, or trusted personal referrals (Chapter 16)

□ Verify no disciplinary history through state bar records for each candidate

□ Schedule initial consultations with at least two candidates

□ Bring asset inventory and list of decisions already made to each consultation

□ Ask the questions from the Chapter 16 attorney vetting table; evaluate answers

□ Confirm fee structure and scope of services before signing the engagement letter

□ Confirm whether funding is included in the engagement or handled separately

The Attorney Drafts the Documents

□ Confirm the attorney understands all relevant complexities: blended family, SNT, MAPT, cognitive concerns, business interests

□ Review draft documents before signing — verify names, proportions, trustee appointments, beneficiary designations

□ Confirm the pour-over will name the trust correctly

□ Confirm DPOA includes or excludes the provisions appropriate for your parent's situation (Chapter 12)

□ If SNT is included: confirm it is a third-party trust with no Medicaid payback requirement (Chapter 14)

- ☐ If MAPT is included: confirm the five-year lookback timeline is understood and documented (Chapter 8)

- ☐ Raise any concerns or questions before the signing — not after

The Signing

- ☐ Confirm all five documents are being signed at the same session: trust, pour-over will, DPOA, healthcare directive, HIPAA authorization

- ☐ Confirm the attorney is meeting privately with your parents before or during the signing to assess capacity

- ☐ Confirm notarization and witness requirements are met for each document

- ☐ If cognitive concerns exist confirm capacity assessment documentation is in the file (Chapter 11)

- ☐ If video documentation is appropriate: confirm this is arranged in advance (Chapter 11)

- ☐ Obtain certified copies of recorded documents where applicable

- ☐ Obtain a certification of trust for use with financial institutions

PHASE THREE

Funding the Trust

Complete within 30–90 days of signing

Real Estate

- ☐ Confirm attorney is preparing deed(s) to transfer primary residence into trust, OR confirm this is your responsibility
- ☐ For each property: verifying new deed is prepared, signed, and recorded with the correct county recorder's office

- ☐ For out-of-state properties: engage an attorney in each state to prepare a state- compliant deed

- ☐ After recording: verify the recorded deed names the trust (not your parent individually) as owner

- ☐ Notify mortgage servicer of transfer if required (most revocable trust transfers are exempt from due-on-sale)

□ Confirm homestead exemption and property tax exemptions are not affected (verify with county assessor)

Bank and Financial Accounts

□ Contact each bank and credit union to retitle accounts to the trust, or add trust as POD beneficiary

□ Bring trust document or certification of trust to each institution

□ For each account: confirm new account statement reflects trust ownership or updated POD designation

□ Contact each brokerage to retitle investment accounts to trust, or add trust as TOD beneficiary

□ For each account: obtain written confirmation of retitling or beneficiary update from the institution

Beneficiary Designations

□ Update all retirement account beneficiary designations (primary and contingent) as planned (Chapter 10)

□ Do NOT retitle retirement accounts to the trust — use beneficiary designation only

□ If trust is named as retirement account beneficiary: confirm with attorney that trust meets IRS designated beneficiary requirements

□ Update all life insurance beneficiary designations (primary and contingent)

□ Obtain written confirmation of each beneficiary designation update from the institution

□ Update any remaining bank/brokerage POD or TOD designations not already addressed above

Other Assets

□ Personal property: confirm general assignment document is signed and attached to trust

□ Business interests: confirm assignment of interest or other transfer mechanism is completed (check operating agreement first)

□ Vehicles: add TOD designation to title where state law allows, OR confirm vehicle is adequately covered by pour-over will

□ Digital financial accounts: update access credentials in secure document accessible to successor trustee.

Verification

□ Pull current statement or account information for every major account and verify trust is listed as owner or POD/TOD beneficiary

□ Pull county recorder record for primary residence and verify trust is listed as owner on the deed

□ Update asset inventory to reflect new titling and beneficiary designations for every asset

□ Give updated asset inventory to successor trustee and executor

PHASE FOUR

Ongoing Maintenance

Annual review and after any significant life event

Annual Review (Every 12 Months)

□ Review asset inventory — identify any new assets acquired since last review that need to be funded into trust

□ Review all beneficiary designations — confirm all are current and accurate

□ Review trustee and agent appointments — confirm named individuals are still willing and able to serve

□ Review the trust's distribution terms — confirm they still reflect your parent's current wishes

□ If parents are over 73: confirm required minimum distributions from retirement accounts are being taken correctly

□ If Medicaid concern exists track the five-year lookback window relative to any transfers made.

After Any Significant Life Event

- ▯ Death of a named trustee, executor, DPOA agent, or healthcare agent — update all appointments immediately
- ▯ Marriage or remarriage of your parents review and update all documents immediately (Chapter 13)
- ▯ Divorce of your parent — update beneficiary designations and trust terms immediately (Chapter 10)
- ▯ Death of a named beneficiary — review distribution terms and contingent designations
- ▯ New property purchased — deed into trust immediately
- ▯ New financial account opened — retitle to trust or add POD/TOD immediately
- ▯ Significant change in your parent's health — review urgency of any incomplete planning
- ▯ Significant change in a family member's circumstances (addiction, divorce, disability) review trust provisions
- ▯ Move to a new state — confirm estate plans that meets new state's requirements
- ▯ Substantial change in estate value (up or down) review whether plan structure still fits.

If Cognitive Decline Becomes a Concern

- ▯ Assess remaining legal capacity urgently — consult elder law attorney within days, not weeks (Chapter 11)
- ▯ Prioritize DPOA and healthcare directive execution if not yet complete
- ▯ Confirm HIPAA authorization is in place and all relevant medical providers have a copy
- ▯ Implement financial account monitoring: transaction alerts, account visibility for trusted family members
- ▯ Review financial exploitation risk and consider structural protections in trust (Chapter 12)
- ▯ Document all significant financial and care decisions in writing at the time

they occur

Where to Store Documents and Who Needs Access

Document	Where to Store	Who Else Needs Access
Original trust document	Fireproof home safe or attorney's vault	Successor trustee (copy); attorney (original or copy)
Pour-over will	With the trust document	Executor; successor trustee
Durable power of attorney	With the trust; a copy with the DPOA agent	Agent named in DPOA — they need it immediately upon incapacity
Healthcare directive	With the trust; a copy with the healthcare agent; a copy in medical records	Healthcare agent; primary care physician; any hospital likely to treat your parent
HIPAA authorization	With healthcare directive, copy with each named authorized person	All named authorized recipients; primary care physician
Asset inventory	Fireproof safe; copy with successor trustee; copy with attorney	Successor trustee; executor — they will need it immediately
Digital account credentials	Password manager with shared master access, or sealed envelope in safe	Successor trustee; at minimum one other trusted person
Beneficiary designation records	With asset inventory; copies of confirmation letters from each institution	Successor trustee; executor

A document nobody can find is functionally no different from a document that doesn't exist. The successor trustee, the DPOA agent, and the healthcare agent all need to be able to locate the relevant documents quickly — often under pressure, often without your parent's assistance. Getting the storage and access right is the last step in the planning process, and it is the step that most directly determines whether the plan can be executed when it needs to be.

Two copies of critical documents should exist in two different physical locations. The original or a certified copy should be stored in a fireproof location — a home safe rated for documents, a bank safe deposit box, or with the estate planning attorney. A second copy should be with the person most likely to need it first: the successor trustee, the DPOA agent, the healthcare agent.

> ***Safe deposit box caution:*** *A safe deposit box is a secure storage location, but it has one significant limitation: if access requires the deceased person's presence and no one else is authorized, the family may need a court order to open it. If a safe deposit box is used to store estate documents, ensure that the successor trustee or another trusted person is authorized on the box while your parent is alive and able to add them.*

Digital Access: What Needs to Be Documented

Digital accounts present a unique access problem. Unlike a bank account where the successor trustee can present legal authority and gain access with patience and proper documentation, many digital platforms have no clear process for account access by family members or legal representatives. Cryptocurrency held in a private wallet is entirely unrecoverable without the private keys. Email accounts with two-factor authentication become inaccessible if no one has the recovery codes. Family photos stored in a cloud service may be behind barriers that take months to navigate.

The solution is documentation, done now, stored securely. The table below covers the digital account categories that create the most access problems and what needs to be documented for each.

Account Type	What to Document	What Happens Without It
Online banking and investment accounts	Institution, username, password, 2FA method	Accounting may be inaccessible; assets delayed reaching successor trustee
Email accounts	Provider, username, password; instructions for what to do with account	Financial and legal correspondence locked away; recovery difficult
Social media profiles	Platform, username, password; preference for memorialization or deletion	Profile remains active indefinitely; family cannot memorialize or remove it
Photo storage (iCloud, Google Photos, etc.)	Service name, login credentials, instructions for downloading or sharing	Family photos locked behind account recovery barriers for months
Cryptocurrency	Exchange accounts OR wallet addresses and seed phrases — both required	Assets are permanently unrecoverable without private keys or seed phrases
Subscriptions with auto-billing	Service names, billing amounts, cancellation instructions	Charges continue against estate funds; executor must track and cancel individually

The most practical storage solution for digital credentials is a password manager with a designated emergency access feature — most major password managers allow a trusted person to request access after a waiting period, during which the account holder can deny the request if they are still active. Alternatively, a written list of critical credentials stored in a sealed envelope in the fireproof safe, with the successor trustee told of its existence and location, works for less tech-comfortable families.

> ***Cryptocurrency is different:*** *Unlike other digital assets, cryptocurrency held in a self-custody wallet is irretrievably lost if the private key or seed phrase is not documented and accessible. There is no customer service number, no account recovery process, no court order that can recover it. If your parent holds any meaningful amount of cryptocurrency, the seed phrase documentation is among the most urgent items on this entire checklist.*

When This Checklist Is Complete

When every item on this checklist is checked off, your parent's estate is planned, documented, funded, and organized in a way that gives their appointed people the authority and information they need to act on their behalf, in any scenario, without court intervention and without uncertainty about what the plan is.

That is a meaningful thing to accomplish. It is also not something most families manage to do all at once. The typical pattern is phases: the conversation happens, then the attorney engagement, then funding which takes weeks or months, then ongoing maintenance that should happen annually but often slips.

Progress matters more than perfection. A trust that is 80 percent funded is enormously better than one that is 0 percent funded. Beneficiary designations that are 90 percent current are vastly better than ones that haven't been reviewed since 2008. Every item completed is protection that didn't exist before.

Use this checklist to track where you are. Return to it. Update it. Share it with the successor trustee and the executor so they know what was done and when. The checklist itself, kept with the estate documents and marked with completion dates, becomes part of the record that helps everyone who comes after.

Chapter 18 addresses what happens when the plan needs to change — the life events that require immediate updates, how often to review, and the one mistake that makes an outdated trust worse than no trust at all.

PART SIX: AFTER THE PLAN IS IN PLACE

Maintaining, Updating, and Executing the Estate

CHAPTER 18

When the Plan Needs to Change

An estate plan is not a document you sign and forget. Life changes. People die, remarry, move, acquire assets, lose capacity, and drift apart in ways that leave outdated plans pointing in the wrong direction. This chapter covers when to update, what to look for, and the one failure mode that makes a neglected trust worse than no trust at all.

Plans Drift. Life Doesn't Wait.

The families who get estate planning most right are not necessarily the ones who create the most sophisticated plan at the outset. They are the ones who treat the plan as a living document that reflects their actual circumstances — updated when circumstances change, reviewed regularly when they haven't, and trusted by the people who need to use it because it was maintained.

An estate plan drafted in 2015 for a parent who was married, owned one home, had three adult children, and held a modest retirement account may be functionally obsolete by 2025 if any of the following have occurred: a spouse died, a child had a major life change, a new property was purchased, the retirement account tripled in value, one of the named trustees moved across the country, or federal estate tax law changed. None of those changes automatically update the plan. Someone has to look at it.

The practical reality is that most families do not look at the estate plan again after the signing. The document goes into the safe, the attorney's file, or a drawer, and it is not touched for years. This is the norm. It is also the condition that produces the outcomes this book exists to prevent: a trust that was appropriate when drafted and is now a liability because it no longer fits.

> *An estate plan that was right ten years ago and wrong today doesn't fail slowly. It fails all at once, when someone dies, and the documents say something that nobody intended anymore.*

The Life Events That Require Immediate Action

Some changes to the estate plan can wait for the next scheduled review. Others cannot. The table below identifies the life events that require immediate attention, events where delay between the change and the plan update creates real legal and financial risk.

Life Event	What to Update Immediately	What to Review
Your parent remarries	All beneficiary designations; trustee appointments	Trust structure for blended family; DPOA and healthcare agent; property titling
Your parent divorces	All beneficiary designations naming ex-spouse; DPOA agent; healthcare agent	Trust distribution terms; trustee appointments; any jointly held property
A named trustee, executor, or agent dies	Replace the appointment before another triggering event occurs	Remaining succession order; whether backup still appropriate
A named beneficiary dies	Per stirpes provisions or contingent designations for that beneficiary's share	Whether distribution intent for that share still reflects parent's wishes

Parents buy new property or opens new accounts	Fund new asset into trust or add beneficiary designation immediately	Asset inventory; overall funding completeness
Parents move to a different state	Healthcare directive (state-specific requirements vary significantly)	DPOA validity; trust recognition; property deed requirements; state tax exposure
A beneficiary develops addiction, disability, or financial crisis	Consider trust provisions for that beneficiary's share	Whether outright distribution is still appropriate; SNT if new disability
Significant change in estate value (up or down)	Review whether plan structure still fits estate size	Tax planning; whether sub-trusts or bypass trust are now warranted or no longer needed
Parents' health declines significantly	Confirm all documents are signed, funded, and accessible	Medicaid timeline; successor trustee readiness; care coordination plan

The remarriage row sits at the top of that table for a reason. A parent who remarries and does not update their estate plan within weeks has potentially created a blended family estate planning crisis in slow motion. Beneficiary designations that name a deceased first spouse still need updating. Trust distribution terms that assumed one spouse may no longer serve a remarried family's goals. A DPOA agent who was the first spouse's sibling may now be inappropriate. None of this update themselves.

The state moves row surprises many families. Most trusts are recognized across state lines without issue, but healthcare directives are the exception — state-specific requirements for advance directives vary enough that a directive signed in one state may not be recognized or easily acted upon in another. A parent who moves to Florida from Massachusetts, or to California from Texas, should have their healthcare directive reviewed and potentially re-executed in compliance with the new state's form and requirements.

> ***The first phone call after any major life event:*** *Call the estate planning attorney and describe what changed. Ask specifically: does this require an amendment, a restatement, or just a beneficiary designation update? The answer varies by event, and the attorney can tell you in a fifteen-minute call what would otherwise take weeks of uncertainty to figure out.*

The Scheduled Review: What to Look for Every Three Years

Beyond responding to specific triggering events, a proactive review of the state plans every two to three years catches the drift that accumulates without any single obvious trigger. Relationships change. Asset values shift. Tax law evolves. People's circumstances change in ways that make their suitability for the roles they've been named different from what it was when they were appointed.

A scheduled review does not necessarily require an attorney appointment. Many of the questions can be evaluated by the family first, with an attorney engaged only if something needs to change.

Trustee and agent appointments

Go through every named appointment in the trust and supporting documents. The successor trustee. The backup successor trustee. The DPOA agent. The healthcare agent. The executor of the pour-over will. For each person, ask: are they still alive? Still willing to serve? Still capable? Still the right person given how circumstances have changed?

A named trustee who has developed their own serious health problems, moved to another country, or had a significant falling out with the family may no longer be appropriate for the role even if nothing has formally changed. A healthcare agent who no longer shares the parent's values about end-of-life care may not execute the parent's wishes the way the parent intends. These are not automatic disqualifications, but they are conversations worth having explicitly.

Any named appointment that is no longer appropriate needs to be updated through a formal trust amendment. This is not optional paperwork. A trustee who is listed in the document but is no longer the right choice will be the legal trustee until the document is changed, regardless of what the family has discussed informally.

Beneficiary designations

Pull the current beneficiary designation forms from every account that has one: retirement accounts, life insurance policies, bank accounts with POD designations, brokerage accounts with TOD designations. Verify that each primary designation is current, that each contingent designation exists and is appropriate, and that no designation names a deceased person, an ex-spouse, or a minor child directly.

This review catches the most common and most costly estate planning failure at the most opportune time — before it matters. A beneficiary designation review that takes an afternoon and finds nothing wrong is time well spent. A beneficiary designation that wasn't reviewed and turns out to name a deceased first spouse costs the family probate, legal fees, and potentially an outcome nobody intended.

Asset inventory and trust funding

Compare the current asset inventory against the assets held in or directed to the trust. Every asset acquired since the trust was last funded needs to be evaluated: is it in the trust, does it have a beneficiary designation, or does it need to be addressed? A new bank account opened for convenience that is now holding $80,000 may still be titled in the parent's individual name without anyone having noticed.

The funding review is where the gap between "we have a trust" and "our trust is working" is either confirmed or discovered. Do this review every time, not just at the beginning.

Distribution terms

Read through the trust's distribution provisions with current circumstances in mind. Does the plan still reflect what your parents want today? A trust that left everything to three adult children equally was appropriate when it was drafted. If one of those children has developed a serious addiction, the distribution terms may no longer serve your parent's actual intentions. If a grandchild has been born and your parents want to include them, the trust may not do that automatically. Distribution terms are the hardest part of the trust to keep current because they require thinking through scenarios rather than just checking boxes. Take time with this section of the review.

Tax law changes

Federal estate and gift tax law changes with legislation, and those changes can significantly affect whether the structure of an existing plan is still optimal. The estate tax exemption level, the gift tax annual exclusion, the rules governing retirement account distributions, and the stepped-up basis rules have all changed in meaningful ways over the past decade and are likely to change again.

A family that planned when the federal exemption was $5 million per person may now have a plan that over-protects assets through bypass trust structures that are no longer necessary at current exemption levels. A family that planned when the stretch IRA was available has a plan that assumed a distribution timeline that no longer exists for most beneficiaries. These are not failures — they are the natural consequence of law changing after planning occurred. The response is a review with an attorney who can assess whether the current structure still serves the family's goals under current law.

How to Amend a Trust vs. Restate It

When the review identifies something that needs to change, the question becomes how to make that change correctly. Two options exist: an amendment and a restatement.

Trust amendment

A trust amendment is a separate document that modifies specific provisions of the existing trust without replacing the whole thing. It is appropriate when the changes are limited — replacing a named trustee, updating a specific distribution provision, adding a new sub-trust for a changed beneficiary circumstance. An amendment is typically faster and less expensive than a full restatement.

The risk with amendments is accumulation. A trust that has been amended five times over fifteen years with five separate amendment documents is technically valid but practically difficult to administer. The successor trustee must read and reconcile five documents to understand the complete plan, and the risk of inconsistency between the original trust and its amendments increases with each successive document. When amendments start to pile up, it is usually time for a restatement.

Trust restatement

A trust restatement replaces the entire body of the original trust document with a new version, while retaining the original trust's identity, name, and date. Because the trust entity itself does not change — only its terms, assets that are already titled in the trust's name do not need to be retransferred. The restatement is a comprehensive update that addresses all necessary changes in a single, clean document.

A restatement is appropriate when multiple changes are needed simultaneously, when the original trust is outdated enough that piecemeal amendment would be unwieldy, or when the plan needs to be significantly restructured rather than adjusted. It costs more than a simple amendment but produces a cleaner, more administrable document.

> ***Rule of thumb:*** *If the changes needed can be captured in one or two targeted amendments and the resulting documents will be easy for a successor trustee to read together, amend. If the trust needs three or more amendments, if the changes are substantial enough to affect multiple sections, or if the existing document is more than ten years old, a restatement is usually the better investment.*

The Outdated Trust That Causes More Problems Than No Trust

This is the situation where this chapter was written around, and it deserves direct attention.

An outdated trust is not just a plan that could be better. In specific circumstances, it is a plan that actively makes things worse. A trust that names a deceased person as successor trustee leaves no functioning trustee — the family must petition the court to appoint one, which costs time and money and requires exactly the court involvement the trust was created to avoid. A trust that directs assets to a deceased beneficiary without stirpes language may leave a share of the estate in legal limbo. A trust that was structured around a bypass trust threshold that made sense under old tax law may now impose administrative complexity with no corresponding tax benefit.

The bypass trust issue is worth explaining specifically because it affects families who planned well at the time but haven't revisited since the Tax Cuts and Jobs Act of 2017 dramatically raised the federal estate tax exemption.

Before 2017, the federal estate tax exemption was low enough that middle-class families with modest assets were genuinely at risk of estate tax exposure. Bypass trusts — also called credit shelter trusts — were a standard planning tool that kept assets below the exemption threshold by splitting the estate between a trust for the surviving spouse and the surviving spouse's own assets. At the first death, assets poured into the bypass trust and were essentially frozen there until the second death, at which point they passed to the children without estate tax.

The problem: assets in a bypass trust do not receive a stepped-up basis at the second death. They were locked in at the basis from the first death. Under current exemption levels, where most families face no federal estate tax exposure, the bypass trust achieves nothing in tax savings while costing the heirs the stepped-up basis benefit on whatever is held in it. The family that planned thoughtfully in 2010 now has a plan that costs their heirs money without providing any corresponding benefit.

> ***Check for bypass trust provisions:*** *If your parent's trust was drafted before 2018 and includes an A-B trust structure, bypass trust provisions, or a credit shelter trust, have an elder law attorney review whether those provisions still serve the family's interests under current exemption levels. The answer depends on the estate size and state-level tax exposure, but the review is worth having.*

When State Law Changes Affect Existing Documents

State laws governing estate planning documents change, and those changes can affect documents that were valid when signed. Healthcare directive requirements, DPOA statutory forms, trust recognition rules, Medicaid eligibility thresholds, and beneficiary designation laws all vary by state and evolve over time.

Most changes to state law are prospective — they affect new documents more than existing ones, which are typically grandfathered under the law in effect when they were executed. But there are exceptions, and there are also practical considerations that extend beyond strict legal validity.

A healthcare directive that was valid under the law in effect ten years ago may be technically valid today but may not use the specific language that hospitals and medical providers in the current environment are familiar with. A DPOA that does not include certain statutory language that has since been added to the state's standard form may be questioned by financial institutions that have updated their acceptance policies to expect the newer form. Legal validity and practical usability are not always the same thing.

The simplest approach is to re-execute healthcare directives and DPOAs every five to seven years or whenever the family moves to a new state, using the current statutory forms. These documents are not complex, and re-execution is inexpensive. The protection it provides against a reluctant hospital or skeptical bank is worth the administrative effort.

When moving to a new state

A trust created in one state is recognized in all states, but the laws of the new state may affect how it is administered, how real estate held in the trust is treated, and what tax exposure it creates. Property purchased in a new state needs a deed prepared under that state's recording requirements. State tax exposure may change depending on where your parents move.

A move to a new state is one of the life events that warrants a full attorney consultation, not just a check-in. Bring the existing plan and a list of assets to an elder law attorney in the new state within the first year of the move.

Keeping the Successor Trustee Ready

One of the most overlooked aspects of estate plan maintenance is keeping the named successor trustee genuinely prepared to perform the role. A successor trustee who has not looked at the trust documents since being named, who does not know where the originals are stored, who has not been updated on changes in the asset inventory, and who has never had the plan explained to them in practical terms is not a functioning successor trustee. They are a name on a piece of paper.

The successor trustee does not need to memorize the trust or become an estate planning expert. They need to know where the documents are, how to reach the estate planning attorney, what assets are in the trust and where statements are stored, what their immediate responsibilities are at incapacity or death, and that they can and should engage professionals to help them through the process. That briefing takes an hour. Not having it can cause weeks of confusion at the worst possible time.

Make it a practice to sit down with the successor trustee every few years — or immediately after any significant update to the plan — and walk them through the current state of the plan. Where the documents are. What the assets are. Who is the attorney? What the immediate next steps are if something happens. This is not a burden on the successor trustee. It is the information they need to do the job your parents trust them to do.

> ***A useful document:*** *Some families prepare a one-page "successor trustee orientation" summary: where the trust is stored, the attorney's contact information, a brief list of major assets and where statements are held, and the three immediate steps the trustee should take when they first assume the role. This document lives with the trust and gets updated whenever the plan is reviewed. It costs nothing to create*

and is worth significantly more than nothing to the person who needs it.

The Annual Review as a Family Practice

The families that maintain their estate plans most effectively are not necessarily the ones where a single organized person takes responsibility for everything. They are the ones where the annual review has become a family practice — a conversation that happens with some regularity, that involves the right people, and that produces concrete action when action is needed.

This does not require a formal family meeting. It can be a phone call between the adult children after Thanksgiving, a question asked during a regular visit, or a standing reminder on the calendar set for the same month each year. What matters is that it happens and that it produces answers to specific questions: has anything changed? Do all the documents still reflect what we intend? Is the trust funded? Are the designations current?

If the answer to all of those questions is yes, the review takes twenty minutes and produces peace of mind. If the answer to any of them is no, the review produces an action item that can be addressed before it becomes a problem rather than after.

A family that builds this practice is doing something more than maintaining a legal document. They are demonstrating to their aging parents that the plan is being taken seriously, that the responsibilities accepted by trustees and agents are being honored, and that the work done to create the plan is being respected rather than neglected. That is not a small thing.

The Plan That Stays Current

The estate plan created at the end of a thoughtful planning process is a snapshot of your parent's life at a specific moment. Keeping it, current means taking that snapshot again, periodically, and updating the plan when the picture has changed enough to matter.

The effort required to maintain a plan is a fraction of the effort required to create one. An annual review that finds nothing to change takes an hour. An update prompted by a life event takes a few weeks and a few hundred dollars. A trust restatement after a decade of significant changes takes two or three attorney meetings and a few thousand dollars. All of these are smaller by orders of magnitude than the cost of discovering, after a death, that the plan no longer reflects reality.

Chapter 19 covers the final phase: what happens after a parent passes. The successor trustee's responsibilities. How assets are distributed. What probate looks like even with a trust. And how to navigate the grief and the paperwork at the same time without letting either one destroys the other.

CHAPTER 19

When a Parent Passes: What Happens Next

Everything in this book has been about preventing a crisis. This chapter is for the moment after one arrives anyway, when a parent has died and the successor trustee, the executor, and the family must navigate grief and legal responsibility at the same time. It is a practical guide to what happens next, what sequence things happen in, and how to keep the family intact through the hardest part.

What the First Days Actually Look Like

When a parent dies, the emotional and the administrative arrive simultaneously. There is no grace period where grief gets to happen first and the legal responsibilities wait.

Social Security needs to be notified. The bank needs a death certificate. Financial institutions that were sending automatic payments will keep sending them until someone calls. And somewhere in that first week, the successor trustee needs to locate the trust document and begin understanding what their role requires.

This is what the planning was for. A family with a funded trust, a current asset inventory, and a successor trustee who has been briefed on their responsibilities is not scrambling in those first days. They know where the documents are. They know who the attorney is. They know what the first steps are. The grief is still grief. But the administrative piece is manageable rather than overwhelming, because someone, at some point, did the work this book describes.

A family without that preparation faces both simultaneously: the emotional weight of loss and the urgent practical problem of figuring out what they own, where it is, who has authority to access it, and what the law requires them to do before they can distribute anything to anyone. The contrast between these two experiences is the clearest possible illustration of what thoughtful planning delivers.

> *The successor trustee's job is not to grieve less. It is to have enough structure that the grief and the administration don't destroy each other.*

The Successor Trustee's Responsibilities: A Sequence

The successor trustee's role activates at death. Their legal authority to act on behalf of the trust begins the moment they assume the role, and their fiduciary duty is the legal obligation to act in the beneficiaries' best interest rather than their own begins at the same moment.

The sequence of responsibilities below represents a standard estate administration timeline for a trust-based estate. Complex estates with business interests, multi-state property, creditor disputes, or tax complications — will have additional steps and will typically require closer attorney involvement throughout.

Timeframe	Trustee Responsibilities	Who Else Is Involved
First 48–72 hours	Obtain death certificates (order at least 10–15 certified copies). Secure the home and any valuables. Locate the trust document and asset inventory. Notify the estate planning attorney.	Funeral home; estate planning attorney
First two weeks	Notify Social Security of the death (benefits must stop; overpayments must be returned). Contact each financial institution to begin retitling or distribution process. Confirm year-of-death RMD has been taken if applicable.	Attorney; CPA; financial institutions
First month	Inventory all trust assets and their current values. Identify and notify all creditors. Cancel subscriptions, memberships, and recurring services. Forward mail.	Attorney; CPA; financial institutions

	Notify Medicare, Medicaid, and any benefit programs.	
One to three months	Pay legitimate debts and creditor claims from estate assets. File the decedent's final income tax return (due April 15 of the following year). File estate income tax return if the estate earns income during administration. Prepare accounting if required by the trust.	CPA; attorney
Distribution	Distribute remaining assets to beneficiaries per terms of trust. Obtain receipts from each beneficiary acknowledging distribution. Close trust accounts after distribution are complete. File final trust accounting if required.	Attorney; CPA; beneficiaries

The single most important early action is obtaining an adequate number of death certificates. Every financial institution, every government agency, every transfer of titled property will require an original certified copy. Running out of certified copies mid- process and waiting for additional copies to arrive from the county creates delays that compound frustration. Fifteen copies is not excessive for an estate of any meaningful complexity.

> ***First call to make:*** *The estate planning attorney. Not to ask what to do in general terms, but to notify them of the death, confirm they have the trust on file, and schedule a meeting in the first week to walk through the administration process step by step. A good attorney will guide the trustee through the sequence, anticipate complications, and handle the legal work the trustee shouldn't be doing alone.*

What a Funded Trust Actually Produces at Death

The difference between settling an estate with a funded trust and settling one without is not abstract. It shows up in months saved, fees avoided, privacy maintained, and family relationships that don't fracture under the pressure of a court process.

	With a Funded Trust	Without a Trust (Probate)
Timeline to distribute assets	Weeks to a few months for most assets	6 months to 2+ years depending on state and complexity
Cost	Attorney fees for trust administration, typically $2,000–$5,000 for a standard estate	Probate fees 3–8% of gross estate value, plus court costs and delays
Privacy	Private — trust terms and asset distribution are not public record	Public — the will, inventory, and distribution are court records anyone can access
Court involvement	None for trust assets	Mandatory court supervision for the duration of probate
Creditor exposure window	Shorter — no public notice requirement in most states	Mandatory creditor notice period in all states; claims can delay distribution
Ability to contest	More difficult to challenge — trust has higher evidentiary standard	Will contests are easier to initiate and more disruptive
Multi-state property	Trust handles all states simultaneously	Ancillary probate required in each state where property is located

The timeline difference is the one families feel most viscerally. A beneficiary who needs to access inherited funds to pay their own bills, settle their own affairs, or simply close a chapter cannot wait eighteen months for probate to run its course. A successor trustee who can distribute assets within weeks of death, because the trust controls the assets and no court is involved, gives beneficiaries something that probate cannot: access when it matters.

The cost difference is significant on any estate worth protecting. Probate fees calculated as a percentage of gross estate value — in some states calculated on the gross value before debts are subtracted — can consume tens of thousands of dollars on an estate that would have cost a fraction of that to administer through a trust. The irony is that the families who most need to preserve every dollar — who cannot afford to give 5 percent of their parent's estate to probate attorneys and court costs — are often the ones who did not plan, which is precisely when those costs hit hardest.

What Probate Looks Like Even with a Trust

A funded living trust avoids probate for the assets it holds. It does not eliminate probate from the picture entirely. Several categories of assets and circumstances can still trigger probate even when a trust exists, and the successor trustee needs to know what they are.

Assets that never made it into the trust

The most common source of probate in trust-based estates is unfunded or partially funded trusts. A bank account opened after the trust was created and never retitled. A piece of real estate acquired ten years ago that was meant to go into the trust but the deed was never prepared. A vehicle with a title still in the deceased's name. These assets are not governed by the trust. They pass through the deceased's probate estate, which means court involvement, delay, and cost for those specific assets.

The pour-over will catch these assets and directs them into the trust, but they still go through probate to get there. The pour-over will is a safety net, not a prevention mechanism. Prevention was the funding process that was supposed to happen when the trust was created.

Small estate procedures

Most states have simplified procedures for small estates or for specific asset types that fall outside the trust — an affidavit of successor, a small estate declaration, or a simplified court process that takes weeks rather than months. An estate attorney in your parent's state can advise on whether any assets that ended up outside the trust can be handled through these simplified procedures rather than full probate.

Disputes that trigger court involvement

A trust that is contested by a beneficiary who claims it was signed under undue influence, that the grantor lacked capacity, or that its terms are invalid can be brought before a court even though the trust itself was designed to avoid court involvement.

Contested trusts are the exception, not the rule — the documentation practices described in Chapter 11 significantly reduce both the grounds for a challenge and the likelihood of one succeeding. But the possibility exists, and families where there is significant conflict should discuss it with the attorney.

> ***One contested asset vs. the whole estate:*** *A dispute over a specific asset or a specific provision of the trust does not necessarily bring the entire estate into probate. Courts can adjudicate a specific dispute while the trust administers the remainder of the estate. The cost and disruption of a partial challenge is real but typically less than full probate. An attorney who specializes in trust administration can advise on the most efficient path through a disputed situation.*

Distributing Assets: How It Works in Practice

Trust distribution is administratively simpler than probate distribution, but it still requires a deliberate sequence. The successor trustee cannot simply divide everything the day after the funeral. There are obligations that must be honored before distribution can occur.

Settling debts and creditor claims

The trust estate is responsible for the deceased's legitimate debts: final medical bills, credit card balances, any outstanding loans, income taxes owed for the year of death. The successor trustee must identify these obligations, determine which are legitimate, and pay them from estate assets before distributing the remainder to beneficiaries.

This does not mean every creditor who sends a bill gets paid without question. Some claimed debts may be invalid, may have already been paid, or may have been discharged. The trustee has an obligation to pay legitimate debts, not to pay any bill that arrives. An estate attorney can advise on which claims are legitimate and which can be challenged or disregarded.

One obligation that cannot wait: the final income tax return. The trustee is responsible for filing a final 1040 for the deceased for the year of death, due April 15 of the following year. If the estate earns income during the administration period — interest on bank accounts, dividends from investment accounts — an estate income tax return (Form 1041) may also be required. A CPA with estate experience should handle this. It is not a standard tax return and the rules that apply are different from those governing living individuals.

Year-of-death RMD

If your parent was over 73 and taking required minimum distributions from retirement accounts, the year-of-death RMD must be taken before year end if your parent had not already taken it. The beneficiary is responsible for this distribution in the year of death. Missing it triggers a penalty. This is one of those administrative details that falls through the cracks in the chaos of the first weeks and is worth flagging explicitly with the CPA.

Formal distribution

Once debts are settled and taxes are addressed, the trustee distributes the remaining assets to beneficiaries per the trust's terms. Each distribution should be documented — a receipt signed by the beneficiary acknowledging the amount received and releasing the trustee from further obligation with respect to that distribution. This documentation protects the trustee from future claims that they distributed incorrectly.

For assets that cannot be easily divided — a family home, a piece of artwork, a vehicle the trust's terms govern how these should be handled. The trust may direct a specific person to receive the asset, may direct the trustee to sell it and distribute the proceeds, or may leave the method to the trustee's discretion. Where the trust is silent and the beneficiaries disagree, the trustee must make a judgment call ideally with attorney guidance that serves the beneficiaries' collective interests rather than any one person's preference.

The Family Home After a Parent Dies

The family home is almost always the most emotionally loaded asset in the estate, and it is frequently the one where the administration gets complicated. The trust may direct that it be sold and the proceeds divided. It may leave the decision to the trustee's discretion. It may give one beneficiary the right of first purchase at appraised value.

Whatever the terms say, the successor trustee is responsible for implementing them, and that responsibility exists in the context of a family that has complicated feelings about the property.

A parent's home is not just an asset. It is where holidays happened, where everyone grew up, where a lifetime of objects accumulated. Clearing it, valuing it, deciding what to keep and what to sell, and ultimately transferring title to new owners is a process that intersects grief in ways that practical guides often underestimate.

Some practical realities are worth knowing. The home can remain in the trust and continue to be maintained during the administration period — the successor trustee has authority to pay the mortgage, insurance, utilities, and maintenance from trust funds. If a beneficiary wants to live in the home during administration, the trustee should formalize that arrangement in writing, including who pays for what, to avoid disputes later.

Appraisals conducted promptly after death reflect the stepped-up basis value and provide documentation for both tax purposes and fair distribution.

> ***Personal property in the home:*** *The contents of a home — furniture, clothing, dishes, tools, photographs, jewelry, sentimental objects — are often technically covered by a general assignment in the trust but practically require a separate family conversation. Who gets what. What is valuable enough to appraise formally. What goes to charity, what goes to family members, what gets sold. This conversation is worth having before the home is cleared rather than during, when everything is happening at once and emotions are highest.*

Keeping the Family Intact Through the Process

The administration of an estate tests families in ways that the planning process cannot fully anticipate. Siblings who were functional during the planning conversations may become adversarial when money is on the table. Beneficiaries who felt their parent's wishes were reasonable in the abstract may feel different when they are on the receiving end of a distribution that doesn't match their expectation. The successor trustee, who may be a sibling themselves, suddenly has legal authority that other siblings may resent or contest.

The planning done in the earlier chapters reduces these pressures significantly. A trust with clear terms, a well-documented signing, a successor trustee who was chosen carefully and briefed thoroughly, and a family that understood the plan while the parent was alive has far fewer opportunities for conflict than one where everything is being figured out after the fact. But it does not eliminate them.

Transparency as protection

The successor trustee's most effective tool for keeping the family intact is transparency. Keeping all beneficiaries informed of the administration's progress, sharing inventory information, explaining the timeline for distribution, and communicating decisions before they are implemented rather than after these practices reduce the suspicion that fuels conflict. A beneficiary who feels informed and consulted, even when they don't get exactly what they wanted, is far less likely to escalate to litigation than one who feels excluded and managed.

Formal accountings — written reports to all beneficiaries documenting what assets were in the estate, what debts were paid, and what was distributed to whom — are required in some states and best practice in all of them. An accounting provided proactively, without being asked, signals that the trustee is operating with integrity and has nothing to hide. An accounting that must be demanded signals the opposite, regardless of what the numbers show.

When conflict happens anyway

Some families arrive at the estate administration with conflict already embedded. Siblings who have not spoken in years. A beneficiary who believes they were promised something the trust does not reflect. A family member who was excluded from the plan and is angry about it. A step-parent and stepchildren who have competing claims on the same assets.

The successor trustee is not a therapist, a mediator, or a judge. Their job is to administer the trust per its terms, not to resolve the family's underlying dynamics. When conflict rises to the level where it is interfering with administration, the right tool is a professional mediator — a neutral third party who can facilitate a structured conversation — before litigation becomes the only remaining option.

Mediation costs a fraction of what litigation costs, resolves faster, and preserves at least the possibility of a functional family relationship after the dispute is resolved. Litigation wins by exhausting the other side financially and emotionally, which is not a win that leaves anyone better off. If conflict is escalating in an estate administration, bring in a mediator before attorneys start billing adversarially.

The trustee who is also a sibling

Being a sibling and a successor trustee simultaneously is genuinely difficult. The role requires acting in all beneficiaries' interests equally — not in the trustee-sibling's personal interest, not in the interest of siblings they are closer to, not in service of resentments or historical grievances. Every decision gets scrutinized by siblings who know the trustee personally and who may read personal motivations into every administrative judgment.

The best protection for a sibling-trustee is documentation and process. Every significant decision recorded in writing at the time it is made, with the reasoning articulated. Every distribution made according to the trust's terms rather than informal agreements. Every debt payment documented with a receipt. This is not paranoia — it is the practice that allows the trustee to demonstrate, if challenged, that they administered the trust appropriately rather than in their own interest.

Closing the Estate

When the debts are settled, the taxes are filed, and the distributions have been made, the trust administration concludes. The successor trustee's role ends. The accounts are closed. The legal entity of the trust, if it was a simple revocable trust rather than an ongoing trust with continuing purposes, ceases to operate.

The final accounting a complete record of everything received, everything paid out, and everything distributed — should be prepared and provided to all beneficiaries. Their signatures acknowledging receipt of the accounting and releasing the trustee from further obligation provide the trustee with protection against future claims. An attorney can prepare the release documents and advise on what the accounting should include.

Keep records for several years after closing. Tax authorities can audit estate tax returns, income tax returns for the year of death, and trust income tax returns for years after the estate is closed. A beneficiary who raises a concern about the administration two years after closing needs to be met with documentation, not memory. The trustee's file should survive the administration itself.

> ***What to preserve:*** *The signed trust document. All amendments or restatements. The death certificate. The final asset inventory and its valuations. Records of every debt paid and every distribution made. The final tax returns. Beneficiary acknowledgment and release forms. Keep these for at least seven years after the estate closes — longer if any aspect of the administration was disputed.*

What This Process Looks Like When the Plan Was in Place

It is worth pausing, at the end of this chapter and the end of this book, to describe what the administration process looks like for a family that did the work.

The parent died with a fully funded revocable living trust. The asset inventory was current and the successor trustee had been briefed on their responsibilities the previous year. The estate planning attorney was called within the first 48 hours. Fifteen certified death certificates were ordered. Social Security was notified within the week.

Over the following six weeks, the attorney guided the trustee through the retitling of financial accounts, the transfer of the family home to the named beneficiaries, and the settlement of final debts. A CPA filed the final income tax return and confirmed that the estate income tax return was not required given the timeline. The year-of-death RMD had already been taken earlier in the year.

Eight weeks after the death, the trustee distributed assets to three adult children per the trust's terms, obtained signed receipts from each, and provided a final accounting. The family met once more to clear and sell the family home an emotional process, but one that proceeded without legal disputes because the trust's terms were clear and everyone understood them.

The total cost of administration: approximately $4,000 in attorney fees, $800 in CPA fees, and $200 in miscellaneous costs. The process took eight weeks from death to final distribution. The family remained intact.

That is what this book was written to make possible.

The End of One Thing and the Beginning of Another

The death of a parent is not an administrative problem to be solved. It is a loss that reorganizes the family, closes a chapter, and leaves everyone who loved that person changed in ways they may not fully understand for years. No estate plan eliminates any of that. Planning is not the antidote to grief.

What planning does is ensure that the grief happens without being compounded by preventable chaos. The family that spends the weeks after a parent's death managing a clear process, honoring a plan the parent put in place, and distributing assets according to terms everyone understood is still grieving. They are just not in crisis.

That distinction between grief that is allowed to be grief and grief that is buried under administrative chaos, legal disputes, and financial uncertainty is the real argument for everything in this book. Not the probate fees saved, not the taxes avoided, not the legal fees prevented, though all those matters. The real argument is that the people your parents love deserve to grieve without fighting. That the successor trustee your parents chose deserves to honor that role without drowning. That the siblings who came together around a parent in their final years deserve to stay together afterward.

A plan makes that possible. The absence of one makes it harder than it needed to be. The work is worth doing. Start today.

Conclusion: The Greatest Gift Is a Plan

Taking the time to create a solid plan for your family's future is a gift that transcends material wealth. While money can provide comfort, security, and opportunity, it is thoughtful preparation—through wills, living trusts, and clear estate planning—that offers peace of mind. For aging parents, it ensures their wishes are respected and their legacy is protected. For their children, it provides clarity, avoiding unnecessary stress and potential conflict down the road. This work is about more than just securing assets; it's about safeguarding the family's values, relationships, and peace of mind. The greatest gift you can give your loved ones is a plan that will carry them through the most challenging times, with dignity and unity intact.

I have a BONUS for You

Thank you for reading ***Don't Let the State Decide***. As a special thank you, I'm offering an exclusive bonus that will enhance your estate planning journey. Simply scan the QR code below to access valuable resources, tools, and additional content designed to help you protect your family's legacy.

Don't miss out on this opportunity, **scan the code now** and start planning with confidence!

www.ingramcontent.com/pod-product-compliance
Lightning Source LLC
LaVergne TN
LVHW080048210926
848481LV00011B/3301
9798233645044